HOW TO FILE FOR DIVORCE IN PENNSYLVANIA

Third Edition

Rebecca A. DeSimone
Edward A. Haman
Attorneys at Law

SPHINX® PUBLISHING
AN IMPRINT OF SOURCEBOOKS, INC.®
NAPERVILLE, ILLINOIS

Third Edition, 2002

Published by: **Sphinx® Publishing, An Imprint of Sourcebooks, Inc.®**

<u>Naperville Office</u>
P.O. Box 4410
Naperville, Illinois 60567-4410
630-961-3900
Fax: 630-961-2168
http://www.sourcebooks.com
http://www.sphinxlegal.com

This publication is designed to provide accurate and authoritative information in regard to the subject matter covered. It is sold with the understanding that the publisher is not engaged in rendering legal, accounting, or other professional service. If legal advice or other expert assistance is required, the services of a competent professional person should be sought.

From a Declaration of Principles Jointly Adopted by a Committee of the American Bar Association and a Committee of Publishers and Associations

This product is not a substitute for legal advice.

Disclaimer required by Texas statutes.

Library of Congress Cataloging-in-Publication Data
DeSimone, Rebecca A., 1963-
 How to file for divorce in Pennsylvania / Rebecca A. DeSimone, Edward A. Haman.--
3rd ed.
  p. cm.-- (Legal survival guides)
 Includes index.
 ISBN 1-57248-211-7 (alk. paper)
  1. Divorce suits--Pennsylvania--Popular works. 2. Divorce suits--Pennsylvania--Forms.
I. Haman, Edward A. II. Title. III. Series.

KFP100.Z9 D47 2002
346.74801'66--dc21
                                          2001057813

Printed and bound in the United States of America.

VHG Paperback — 10 9 8 7 6 5 4 3 2 1

CONTENTS

Using Self-Help Law Books

Before using a self-help law book, you should realize the advantages and disadvantages of doing your own legal work and understand the challenges and diligence that this requires.

THE GROWING TREND

Rest assured that you won't be the first or only person handling your own legal matter. For example, in some states, more than seventy-five percent of divorces and other cases have at least one party representing him or herself. Because of the high cost of legal services, this is a major trend and many courts are struggling to make it easier for people to represent themselves. However, some courts are not happy with people who do not use attorneys and refuse to help them in any way. For some, the attitude is, "Go to the law library and figure it out for yourself."

We at Sphinx write and publish self-help law books to give people an alternative to the often complicated and confusing legal books found in most law libraries. We have made the explanations of the law as simple and easy to understand as possible. Of course, unlike an attorney advising an individual client, we cannot cover every conceivable possibility.

COST/VALUE ANALYSIS

Whenever you shop for a product or service, you are faced with various levels of quality and price. In deciding what product or service to buy, you make a cost/value analysis on the basis of your willingness to pay and the quality you desire.

When buying a car, you decide whether you want transportation, comfort, status, or sex appeal. Accordingly, you decide among such choices as a Neon, a Lincoln, a Rolls Royce, or a Porsche. Before making a decision, you usually weigh the merits of each option against the cost.

When you get a headache, you can take a pain reliever (such as aspirin) or visit a medical specialist for a neurological examination. Given this choice, most people, of course, take a pain reliever, since it costs only pennies; whereas a medical examination costs hundreds of dollars and takes a lot of time. This is usually a logical choice because it is rare to need anything more than a pain reliever for a headache. But in some cases, a headache may indicate a brain tumor and failing to see a specialist right away can result in complications. Should everyone with a headache go to a specialist? Of course not, but people treating their own illnesses must realize that they are betting on the basis of their cost/value analysis of the situation. They are taking the most logical option.

The same cost/value analysis must be made when deciding to do one's own legal work. Many legal situations are very straight forward, requiring a simple form and no complicated analysis. Anyone with a little intelligence and a book of instructions can handle the matter without outside help.

But there is always the chance that complications are involved that only an attorney would notice. To simplify the law into a book like this, several legal cases often must be condensed into a single sentence or paragraph. Otherwise, the book would be several hundred pages long and too complicated for most people. However, this simplification necessarily leaves out many details and nuances that would apply to special or unusual situations. Also, there are many ways to interpret most legal questions. Your case may come before a judge who disagrees with the analysis of our authors.

Therefore, in deciding to use a self-help law book and to do your own legal work, you must realize that you are making a cost/value analysis. You have decided that the money you will save in doing it yourself outweighs the chance that your case will not turn out to your satisfaction. Most people handling their own simple legal matters never have a problem, but occasionally people find that it ended up costing them more to have an attorney straighten out the situation than it would have if they had hired an attorney in the beginning. Keep this in mind if you decide to handle your own case, and be sure to consult an attorney if you feel you might need further guidance.

LOCAL RULES The next thing to remember is that a book which covers the law for the entire nation, or even for an entire state, cannot possibly include every procedural difference of every county court. Whenever possible, we provide the exact form needed; however, in some areas, each county, or even each judge, may require unique forms and procedures. In our *state* books, our forms usually cover the majority of counties in the state, or provide examples of the type of form that will be required. In our *national* books, our forms are sometimes even more general in nature but are designed to give a good idea of the type of form that will be needed in most locations. Nonetheless, keep in mind that your *state*, county, or judge may have a requirement, or use a form, that is not included in this book.

You should not necessarily expect to be able to get all of the information and resources you need solely from within the pages of this book. This book will serve as your guide, giving you specific information whenever possible and helping you to find out what else you will need to know. This is just like if you decided to build your own backyard deck. You might purchase a book on how to build decks. However, such a book would not include the building codes and permit requirements of every city, town, county, and township in the nation; nor would it include the lumber, nails, saws, hammers, and other materials and tools you would need to actually build the deck. You would use the book as your guide, and then do some work and research involving such matters as whether you need a permit of some kind, what type and grade of wood are available in your area, whether to use hand tools or power tools, and how to use those tools.

Before using the forms in a book like this, you should check with your court clerk to see if there are any local rules of which you should be aware, or local forms you will need to use. Often, such forms will require the same information as the forms in the book but are merely laid out differently, use slightly different language, or use different color paper so the clerks can easily find them. They will sometimes require additional information.

CHANGES IN THE LAW

Besides being subject to state and local rules and practices, the law is subject to change at any time. The courts and the legislatures of all fifty states are constantly revising the laws. It is possible that while you are reading this book, some aspect of the law is being changed or that a court is interpreting a law in a different way. You should always check the most recent statutes, rules and regulations to see what, if any changes have been made.

In most cases, the change will be of minimal significance. A form will be redesigned, additional information will be required, or a waiting period will be extended. As a result, you might need to revise a form, file an extra form, or wait out a longer time period; these types of changes will not usually affect the outcome of your case. On the other hand, sometimes a major part of the law is changed, the entire law in a particular area is rewritten, or a case that was the basis of a central legal point is overruled. In such instances, your entire ability to pursue your case may be impaired.

To help you with local requirements and changes in the law, be sure to read the section in Chapter 2 on "Legal Research."

Again, you should weigh the value of your case against the cost of an attorney and make a decision as to what you believe is in your best interest.

INTRODUCTION

Going through a divorce is probably one of the most common, and most traumatic, encounters with the legal system. At a time when you are least likely to have extra funds, paying a divorce lawyer can be one of the most expensive bills to pay. In a contested divorce case, it is not uncommon for the parties to run up legal bills of over $10,000. Horror stories abound of lawyers charging substantial fees with little progress to show for it.

This book is designed to enable you to obtain a divorce without hiring a lawyer. Even if you do hire a lawyer, this book will help you to work with him or her more effectively, which can also reduce the legal fees. In addition, this book will provide you with a sound outline to aid you in the understanding of all aspects of divorce in Pennsylvania.

This is not a law school course, but rather a practical guide to move you through "the system" as easily as possible. Most of the legal jargon has been eliminated. For ease of understanding, this book uses the term *spouse* to refer to your husband or wife (whichever applies), and the terms *child* and *children* are used interchangeably. Gender selections have been made for ease of discussion and in no way are meant to suggest preference or standard.

In most counties, divorce cases are filed with the prothonotary's office. However, in some areas, such as Philadelphia, divorce cases are filed with the family court clerk's office. Throughout this book, we will use the word *prothonotary*, which will also mean *clerk* in those counties with a clerk's office, unless otherwise indicated.

Please keep in mind that different judges, and courts in different counties, may have their own particular (if not peculiar) procedures, forms, and ways of doing things. The prothonotary's office (or family court clerk's office in those counties with a family court, such as Philadelphia) often can tell you if they have any special forms or requirements. Personnel at the prothonotary's office cannot give legal advice, but they can tell you what their court or judges require.

The first two chapters of this book will give you an overview of the law and the legal system. Chapter 1 will provide you with a better understanding of the legal elements involved in "marriage." Chapter 2 will take you through a brief analysis of the Pennsylvania legal system. Chapter 3 will help you decide if you want an attorney. Chapters 4 through 6 will help you evaluate your situation and give you an idea of what to expect if you decide to go through with a divorce. Chapter 6 will analyze how you maneuver through the child custody, visitation, and support areas of the legal system. Chapter 7 provides an introduction to the legal forms required in your divorce action. Chapter 8 addresses divorces based upon mutual consent. Chapter 9 explores the simple uncontested divorce. Chapter 10, in contrast, analyzes the contested divorce process. The Master's Hearing process is the focus of Chapter 11. Finally in Chapter 12, specific special circumstances are addressed such as what to do when you cannot afford court costs, how to protect yourself, your children and property and other specific circumstances. The remaining chapters will show you what forms you need, how to fill out the forms, and what procedures to follow. There is a glossary to help you understand many of the legal terms used in this book. You will also find three appendices in the back of the book.

Appendix A contains selected portions of the Pennsylvania law dealing with divorce, property division, alimony, child support, and child custody. Although these provisions are discussed in the book, it is sometimes helpful to read the law exactly as it is written.

Appendix B contains checklists of the documents you may need to prepare and file in various types of divorce procedures.

Appendix C contains the forms you will complete. You will not need to use all of the forms. This book will tell you which forms you need, depending upon your situation, and will guide you in filling in the necessary information.

Philadelphia forms are included in Appendix C for ease of use and to provide clarity for those filing in the Philadelphia system. This book supplies you with instructions for completing general forms related to Philadelphia County. However, since Philadelphia makes use of a very unique, specific, and complicated battery of forms, it is advisable that you contact the Clerk of Courts in Philadelphia County to request particular forms. It is quite common that the forms utilized in this regard are amended frequently and thus, the general forms contained in this book may be rejected if not adapted to appropriately meet Philadelphia requirements.

NOTE: *Be sure to read "An Introduction to Legal Forms" in Chapter 7 before you use any of the forms in this book.*

Marriage "Ins and Outs"

1

Several years (or maybe only months) ago, you made a decision to get married. This chapter will discuss, in a very general way, what you got yourself into, how to get out, and whether you really want to do so.

Marriage

Marriage is frequently referred to as a contract. It is a legal contract, and, for many, it is also a religious contract. This book will deal only with the legal aspects. The wedding ceremony involves the bride and groom reciting certain vows that are actually mutual promises about how they will treat each other. Legal papers are signed, such as a marriage license and a marriage certificate. These formalities create certain rights and obligations for the husband and wife. Although the focus at the ceremony is on the emotional and romantic aspects of the relationship, the legal reality is that financial and property rights are being created. Such financial and property rights and obligations cannot be broken without a legal proceeding.

Marriage will give each of the parties certain rights in property, and it creates certain obligations with respect to the support of any children the parties have together (or adopt). Unfortunately, most people do not fully realize that these rights and obligations are being created until it comes time for a divorce. Pennsylvania does recognize *common law* marriage (marriage caused to exist by co-habitating and holding one's self out to the public as husband and wife). Pennsylvania does not, however, recognize homosexual marriage.

DIVORCE

A divorce is the most common method of terminating or breaking the marriage contract. In a divorce, the court declares the marriage contract broken, divides the parties' property and debts, decides if either party should receive alimony, and determines the support, custody, and visitation with respect to any children the parties may have. Traditionally, a divorce could only be granted under certain very specific circumstances, such as for *adultery* or *mental cruelty*.

Today, a divorce may be granted simply because one or both of the parties want one. The wording used to describe the situation is that *the marriage is irretrievably broken*.

PROCEDURES   There are two ways to file for a divorce in Pennsylvania. The first is under the *no-fault* statute, in which no legal *grounds* for divorce are required. With approximately ninety percent of all persons seeking divorce filing under this section, this is the most commonly utilized method of filing for divorce in Pennsylvania. If both parties agree to a divorce, the process can be completed in as little as ninety-one days. If your spouse will not agree to a divorce, you and your spouse must live *separate and apart* for at least two years before you can obtain a no-fault divorce.

No-fault divorce is typically faster and less expensive than your second option, which is the *fault divorce* or *divorce with grounds*. This process entails proof of very specific events such as adultery, barbarous treatment, fraud, incapacity of the mind, or abandonment. Because proof of these elements is required, fault divorces can become expensive and time consuming and should not generally be attempted without a lawyer. Fault divorces are not covered in detail in this book.

Living Separate and Apart for Two Years

There are two questions that often arise when a divorce is filed on the basis of living separate and apart for two years:

1. What does it mean to live *separate and apart*?
2. When does the two year period begin to run?

Generally, living separate and apart means that you and your spouse are living separate lives, with no intention of ever getting back together. To make it clear that you are truly living separate and apart, most divorce lawyers would advise you to move out of your home, and clearly tell your spouse (in front of a friend or relative who can be a witness) that you never intend to live with him or her again.

The two year period begins to run when you and your spouse separate, with the intention to end your marriage. If your spouse does not object to the date you select, that date will usually be accepted by the court. However, if your spouse does not agree on the date, you will need to prove that you separated on that date. If you cannot prove it, the court will typically go by the date you filed your COMPLAINT IN DIVORCE. (see form 4, p.180.)

The following example shows the type of problems that can arise if it is not made clear that you and your spouse began living separate and apart on a certain date.

Example: Bob moves out, and twenty months later Mary files for divorce, expecting that she will get her divorce decree in about four months when the two year separation period is done. Bob files a response saying that he just moved out because he was seeking business or employment opportunities in another city and always intended to move back in with Mary. The judge rules that there is no evidence that the parties intended to separate at the time Bob moved out. Therefore, the separation period began when Mary filed her COMPLAINT IN DIVORCE. She will have to wait almost two more years before she can get a divorce decree.

There are court cases where a couple has been considered to have lived separate and apart while continuing to live in the same house. In such instances, the couple went to great trouble to separate their lives, such as sleeping in separate bedrooms and maintaining separate food supplies.

There are other cases where a couple did this, and the court determined they were *not* living separate and apart. Such situations offer too much opportunity for your spouse to deny the separation, or for the judge to refuse to accept it, and thereby greatly delay the entry of a DECREE OF DIVORCE. (see form 18, p.199.) In such situations, it is also more difficult to establish the date when the separation began.

ANNULMENT

The basic difference between a divorce and an *annulment* is that a divorce says, "this marriage is broken," and an annulment says, "there never was a marriage." An annulment is more difficult and often more complicated to prove, so it is not used very often. Annulments are only possible in a few circumstances, usually where one party deceived the other. If you decide that you want an annulment, you should consult an attorney. If you are seeking an annulment for religious reasons and need to go through a church procedure (rather than, or in addition to, a legal procedure), you should consult your priest or minister.

Generally, a divorce is easier to obtain than an annulment. This is because all you need to prove to get a divorce is that your marriage is broken. How do you prove this? Simply by saying it. The COMPLAINT IN DIVORCE reads: "The marriage is irretrievably broken." (see form 4, p.180.) That is all you need to do. However, in order to get an annulment, you will need to prove more. This proof will involve introducing various documents into evidence and having other people come to testify at the court hearing.

GROUNDS FOR ANNULMENT

Annulments can only be granted under one of these six circumstances:

1. One of the parties was too young to get married. In Pennsylvania, both parties must be at least eighteen years old to be married (there are a few exceptions, such as where the woman is pregnant or the under-age person has parental consent; but these exceptions only apply if the person is at least sixteen).

2. One of the parties is guilty of fraud. For example, where one party just got married in order to have the right to inherit from the other with no intention of ever living together as husband and wife.

3. One party was under duress when he or she got married. *Duress* means that the person was being threatened, or was under outside pressure, so that he or she did not get married voluntarily.

4. One party did not have the mental capacity to get married. This means the person was suffering from mental illness or disability (such as being severely retarded), to such an extent that the person

did not understand he or she was getting married; or possibly did not even understand the concept of marriage.

5. One party was already married to another person. This might occur if one party married, mistakenly believing the divorce from his or her previous spouse was final.

6. The marriage is incestuous. Pennsylvania law prohibits marriage between certain family members, such as brother and sister, aunt and nephew, or uncle and niece.

If your spouse wants to stop an annulment, there are several arguments he or she could make to further complicate the case. This area of the law is not as well defined as divorce, and annulments are much less common than divorces. The annulment procedure can be extremely complicated and should not be attempted without consulting a lawyer.

LEGAL SEPARATION

Since Pennsylvania is a *common law* marriage state (parties may hold themselves out as husband and wife, and under certain circumstances, be deemed married without a marriage license, certificate, or ceremony), no law of *legal separation* exists. Pennsylvania does not permit a legal separation. This procedure is available in some states, and is used to divide the property and provide for child custody and support in cases where the husband and wife live separately, but remain married. This is usually used to break the financial rights and obligations of a couple whose religion does not permit divorce.

Some states refer to this procedure as *divorce from bed and board*. It is an old procedure that is gradually fading from use. Pennsylvania does provide the ability to obtain child support or alimony, and to determine custody and visitation rights, without getting a divorce, but it does not allow for the division of property. This procedure for child support without divorce, often mistakenly called a legal separation, is beyond the scope of this book.

GETTING A DIVORCE

Divorce will have an impact upon several aspects of your life and can change your entire lifestyle. Before you begin the process of getting a divorce, you need to take some time to think about the way in which it will affect your life. This section will help you examine these aspects and offer alternatives in the event you wish to try to save your relationship. Even if you feel absolutely certain that you want a divorce, you should still read this section so you will be prepared for what may follow.

LEGAL DIVORCE

Legal divorce is the process of breaking your matrimonial bonds—the termination of your marriage contract and partnership. The stress created is that of going through a court system procedure and having to deal with your spouse as you go through it. However, when compared to the other aspects of divorce, the legal divorce does not last very long. On the other hand, the legal divorce can be the most confrontational and emotionally explosive stage.

Generally, there are three matters to be resolved through the legal divorce process:

1. the divorce of two people. This gives each the legal right to marry someone else;

2. the division of their property and responsibility for debts (called equitable distribution); or,

3. the care and custody of their children.

Although it is theoretically possible for the legal divorce to be concluded within a few months, the legalities may continue for years, mostly caused by the emotional aspects leading to battles over the children.

SOCIAL AND EMOTIONAL DIVORCE

Divorce will have a tremendous effect upon your social and emotional lives, which will continue long after you are legally divorced. These effects include:

Lack of companionship. Even if your marriage is one of the most miserable, you may still notice at least a little emptiness or loneliness after the divorce. It may not be that you miss your spouse in particular, but just miss another person being around you.

Grief. Divorce may be viewed as the death of a marriage, or maybe the funeral ceremony for the death of a marriage. Like the death of anyone you have been close to, you will feel a sense of loss. This aspect can take you through all of the normal feelings associated with grief.

You will become angry and frustrated over the years you have "wasted." You will feel guilty because you "failed to make the marriage work." You will find yourself saying, "I cannot believe this is happening to me." For months, or even years, you will spend a lot of time thinking about your marriage. It can be extremely difficult to put it all behind you and to move on with your life.

The single's scene: Dating. You may find that you are dropped from friends' guest lists as your current friends, who are probably all married, no longer find that you as a single person fit in with their circle. If you want to avoid solitary evenings before the TV, you will find yourself trying to get back into the "single's scene." This can be very difficult, especially if you have custody of the children.

FINANCIAL DIVORCE

Many married couples are just able to make ends meet. After divorce there are two rent payments, two electric bills, etc. For the spouse without custody, there is also child support to be paid. For at least one spouse, and often for both, money becomes even tighter than it was before the divorce. Also, once you have divided your property, each of you will need to replace the items the other person was able to keep.

CHILDREN AND DIVORCE

The effect upon your children, and your relationship with them, can often be the most painful and long-lasting aspect of divorce. Your relationship with your children may become strained as they work through their feelings of blame, guilt, disappointment, and anger. This strain may continue for many years. You and your children may even need professional counseling. Also, as long as there is child support and partial custody, shared custody, or visitation involved, you will be forced to have at least some contact with your ex-spouse.

ALTERNATIVES
TO DIVORCE

By the time you have purchased this book, and read this far, you have probably already decided that you want a divorce. However, if what you have just read and thought about has made you want to make a last effort to save your marriage, there are a few things you can try. These are only very basic suggestions. Details, and other suggestions, can be offered by professional marriage counselors.

Talk to your spouse. Choose the right time (not when your spouse is trying to unwind after a day at work, or is trying to quiet a screaming baby), and talk about your problems. Try to establish a few ground rules for the discussion.

- Talk about how you feel, instead of making accusations that may start an argument.

- Each person listens while the other speaks (no interrupting).

- Each person must say something that he or she likes about the other, and about the relationship.

As you talk, you may want to discuss such things as where you would like your relationship to go, how it has changed since you got married, and what can be done to bring you closer together.

Change your thinking. Many people get divorced because they refuse to change something about their outlook or their lifestyle. Then, once they get divorced, they find they have made that very same change they resisted for so long.

Example: George and Wendy were unhappy in their marriage. They did not seem to share the same lifestyle. George felt overburdened with responsibility and bored. He wanted Wendy to be more independent and outgoing, to meet new people, to handle the household budget, and to go out with him more often. However, Wendy was more shy and reserved, was not confident in her ability to find a job and succeed in the business world, and preferred to stay at home. Wendy wished that George would give up some of his frequent nights out with the guys, would help with the cooking and laundry, would stop leaving messes for her to clean up, and would stop bothering her about going out all the time. But neither would try to change, and eventually all of the little things built up into a divorce.

After the divorce, Wendy was forced to get a job to support herself. Now she has made friends at work, she goes out with them two or three nights a week, she is successful and happy at her job, and she is quite competent at managing her own budget. George now has his own apartment and has to cook his own meals (something he finds he enjoys), and do his own laundry. He has also found it necessary to clean up his own messes and keep the place neat, especially if he is going to entertain guests. George has even thought about inviting Wendy over for dinner and a quiet evening at his place. Wendy has been thinking about inviting George out for a drink after work with her friends.

Both George and Wendy have changed in exactly the way the other had wanted. It is just too bad they did not make these changes before they got divorced. If you think some change may help, give it a try. You can always resort to a divorce if the situation does not improve.

Counseling. Counseling is not the same as giving advice. A counselor should not be telling you what to do. A counselor's job is to assist you in figuring out what you really want to do. A counselor will ask questions that will get you thinking. Actually, just talking things out with your spouse is a form of self-counseling. The only problem is that it is difficult to remain objective and non-judgmental. Both of you need to be able to calmly analyze what the problems are and discuss possible solutions.

Very few couples seem to be able to do this successfully, which is why there are professional marriage counselors. As with doctors and lawyers, good marriage counselors are best discovered by word of mouth. You may have friends who can direct you to someone who helped them. Also, you can check with your family doctor or your clergyman for a referral, or even scan the telephone yellow pages under "Marriage and Family Counselors" or some similar category. You can see a counselor either alone or with your spouse. It may be a good idea for you to see a counselor even if you are going through with the divorce.

Another form of individual counseling is talking to a close friend. Remember, however, the difference between counseling and advice giving. Do not let your friend tell you what you should do.

Trial separation. Before going to the time, expense, and trouble of getting a divorce, you and your spouse may want to try just getting away from each other for awhile. This can be as simple as taking separate vacations, or as complex as actually separating into separate households for an indefinite period of time. This may give each of you a chance to think about how you will like living alone, how important or trivial your problems are, and how you really feel about each other.

THE LEGAL SYSTEM 2

This chapter will give you a general introduction to the legal system. There are things you need to know in order to obtain a divorce (or help your lawyer get the job done), and to get through any encounter with the legal system with a minimum of stress. These are some of the realities of our system. If you do not learn to accept these realities, you will experience much stress and frustration.

THEORY VERSUS REALITY

Our legal system is a system of rules. There are three basic types of rules:

1. *Rules of Law*: These are the basic substance of the law, such as a law telling a judge how to go about dividing your property.

2. *Rules of Procedure*: These outline how matters are to be handled in the courts, such as requiring court papers to be in a certain form, or filed within a certain time.

3. *Rules of Evidence*: These set forth the manner in which facts are to be proven.

The theory is that these rules allow each side to present evidence most favorable to that side, and an independent person or persons (the judge or jury) will figure out the truth. Then certain legal principles will be applied to that "truth" which will give a fair resolution of the dispute. These legal principles are supposed to be relatively unchanging so that we can all know what will happen in any given situation and can plan our lives accordingly. This provides order and predictability to our society. Any change in the legal principles is supposed to occur slowly, so that the expected behavior in our society is not confused from day-to-day. Unfortunately, the system does not really work this way. What follows are only some of the problems in the real legal system.

THE SYSTEM IS NOT PERFECT

Contrary to how it may seem, legal rules are not made just to complicate matters and confuse everyone. They are attempts to make the system fair and just. They have been developed over hundreds of years, and in most cases, they make sense. Unfortunately, our efforts to find fairness and justice have resulted in a complex set of rules.

The legal system affects our lives in important ways, and it is not a game. However, it can be compared to a game in some ways. The rules are designed to apply to all people and in all cases. Sometimes, the rules do not seem to provide a fair result in a certain situation, but the rules are still followed. Just as a referee can make a bad call, so can a judge. There are also cases where one side wins by cheating.

JUDGES DO NOT ALWAYS FOLLOW THE RULES

Many young lawyers are shocked to discover that judges do not always follow the rules. After spending three years in law school learning legal theory, and after spending countless hours preparing for a hearing and having all of the law on your side, you find that the judge is not going to pay any attention to legal theories and the law. Many judges are going to make a decision simply on what they think seems fair under the circumstances. This concept is actually being taught in some law schools now.

Unfortunately, what seems fair to a particular judge may depend upon his or her personal ideas and philosophy. For example, there is nothing in the divorce laws that gives one parent priority in child custody; however, many judges believe that a child is generally better off with his or her mother. All other things being equal, these judges will still find a way to justify awarding custody to the mother.

THE SYSTEM IS OFTEN SLOW

Even lawyers get frustrated at how long it can take to get a case completed. Whatever your situation, things will take longer than you expect. Patience is required to get through the system with a minimum of stress. Do not let your frustration show. No matter what happens, keep calm, be courteous, and be patient.

NO TWO CASES ARE ALIKE

Just because your friend's case went a certain way does not mean your case will have the same result. The judge can make a difference, and more often, the circumstances will make a difference. Just because your co-worker makes the same income as you and has the same number of children, you can not assume you will be ordered to pay the same amount of child support. There are usually other circumstances your co-worker does not tell you about, and possibly does not understand.

DIVORCE "SLICES THE PIE"

Remember, there are two sides to every legal issue, so do not expect to have every detail go your way. Whatever the ultimate result, it is always less than the whole picture before the divorce. Viewing your marital status as a "whole pie," divorce results in a "slicing of the pie." Stability, finances, and emotions are all affected. Although any particular matter may not be decided in your favor, the goal is to keep as much of the pie intact as possible. A positive approach is essential.

DIVORCE LAW AND PROCEDURE

Very specific procedures are required in maneuvering through the legal aspects of a divorce. It is critical when undertaking your own representation that you fully comprehend the practices and requirements of the domestic relations arena.

THE PLAYERS

Law and the legal system are often compared to games, and just like games, it is important to know the players.

The judge. The judge has the power to decide whether you can get divorced, how your property will be divided, how custody of the children will be arranged, and how much the other will pay for child support. The judge is the last person you want to make angry.

In general, judges have large caseloads and like it best when your case can be concluded quickly and without hassle. This means that the more you and your spouse agree upon, and the more complete your paperwork, the more you will please the judge. Most likely, your only direct contact with the judge will be at certain hearings, which may last as little as five minutes. (See Chapter 7 for more about how to deal with the judge.)

The judge's secretary. The judge's secretary sets the hearings for the judge and can frequently answer many of your questions about the procedure and what the judge would like or require. Once again, you do not want to make an enemy of the secretary. This means that you do not call the judge's secretary often, and do not ask too many questions. A few questions are acceptable, and you may want to start off saying that you just want to make sure you have everything in order for the judge. You will get much farther by being nice than by arguing.

The master. In most cases, the judge appoints a person, called a *family law master* or simply *master*, to hear divorce cases. This is to help the judges manage the court's case load. The master has virtually the same powers as a judge, and should be treated the same as a judge. Therefore, if you end up needing a hearing, it will probably be before a master instead of a judge. In practical terms, the only difference is in the person's title. You will handle your case the same, regardless of whether you are presenting it to a judge or master. In this book, the words *judge* and *master* are used interchangeably. Any information, advice, or instructions that relate to a judge, also apply to a master.

The court prothonotary or clerk. In most counties in Pennsylvania, divorce cases are filed with the office of the prothonotary (in most states, the prothonotary is called the *court clerk*). In a few places, such as Philadelphia, divorce cases are filed with the office of the family court clerk.

NOTE: *Unless a significant distinction between the prothonotary and clerk is noted, any reference to the* prothonotary *should also be considered as a reference to the* clerk *in those counties.*

Where the secretary usually works for only one judge, the prothonotary handles the files for all of the judges. The prothonotary's office is the central place where all of the court files are kept. The prothonotary files your court papers and keeps the official records of your divorce.

Most people who work in the prothonotary's office are friendly and helpful. While they cannot give you legal advice (such as advising you what to say in your court papers), they can help explain the system and the procedures (such as telling you what type of papers must be filed). The prothonotary has the power to accept or reject your papers, so you do not want to anger the prothonotary. If the prothonotary tells you to change something in your papers, just change it. Do not argue or complain.

Lawyers. Lawyers serve as guides through the legal system. They try to guide their clients and be advocates for them. In dealing with your spouse's lawyer (if he or she has one), try to be polite. You will not get anywhere by being antagonistic. Generally, the lawyer is just doing his or her job to get the best situation for his or her client. If you find you cannot deal with your spouse's attorney, it is a good idea for you to get a lawyer also. Chapter 3 will provide more information to help you decide if you need a lawyer.

This book. This book will serve as your map through the legal system. In most cases, the dangers along the way are relatively small. If you start getting lost, or the dangers seem to be getting worse, you can always hire a lawyer to jump to your aid. You may wish to contact the *Lawyer's Referral Service* in your area. Your county bar association can guide you in this regard.

The following sections will give you a general overview of the law and procedures involved in obtaining a divorce. To most people, including many lawyers, the law appears very complicated and confusing. Fortunately, many areas of the law can be broken down into simple and logical steps. Divorce is one of those areas.

THE LAW   The law relating to divorce, as well as to any other area of law, comes from two sources: 1) the Pennsylvania Statutes, which are the laws passed by the Pennsylvania Legislature and 2) the past decisions of the Pennsylvania court (called *case law*). This book is designed so that you will not need to research the law. However, a portion of the Pennsylvania Statutes, relating to property division, alimony, and child support, can be found in Appendix A of this book.

The past decisions of the Pennsylvania courts are much more difficult to locate and follow. For most situations, the law is clearly spelled out in the statutes, and the past court decisions are not necessary. However, if you wish to learn more about how to find these court decisions, see the section entitled "Legal Research" later in this chapter.

> ### Residency Requirement:
>
> In order for you to file for divorce in any court in Pennsylvania, either you or your spouse must be a resident of Pennsylvania for at least six months immediately before filing a petition with the court. (See Chapter 4 for more details.)

FAULT
GROUNDS FOR
DIVORCE

In Pennsylvania, there are several distinct situations that will allow you to obtain a divorce. These situations are referred to as the *grounds* for divorce. You can still use the traditional grounds for divorce, which are:

- willful and malicious desertion for at least one year;

- adultery;

- cruel and barbarous treatment endangering your life or health;

- knowing bigamy;

- your spouse being sentenced to imprisonment for a period of at least two years;

- your spouse offering such indignities toward you so as to render your condition intolerable and life burdensome (this is similar to what is called *mental cruelty* in many other states); or,

- your spouse suffering from insanity or serious mental disorder that results in his or her confinement to a mental institution for at least eighteen months before you file for divorce, and there is no reasonable prospect of his or her being discharged within eighteen months after you file for divorce.

Divorce using these traditional grounds is not covered by this book. Using any of the above grounds for divorce will complicate the process, and you should therefore hire an attorney.

NO-FAULT
DIVORCE

Pennsylvania has created a more simple legal justification for divorce, commonly known as *no-fault* divorce. This book covers no-fault divorce. A no-fault divorce can be obtained in Pennsylvania in either of two situations. These are:

1. Your marriage is irretrievably broken and you both agree to a divorce.

2. Your marriage is irretrievably broken and you and your spouse have lived separate and apart for at least two years.

The law is simple in most divorce cases. You will need to show the following three points:

1. that your marriage is irretrievably broken (done simply by stating this fact, which means that your marriage relationship is broken and cannot be saved). If your spouse does not agree to the divorce, you will also need to show that you have lived separate and apart for at least two years;

2. how your property should be divided between you and your spouse; and,

3. how custody of your children should be shared, and how they should be supported.

THE
PROCEDURE

As for procedures, the most simple divorce may be viewed as a five-step process:

1. File certain papers with the prothonotary, asking the judge to grant a divorce.

2. Notify your spouse that you are filing for divorce by sending a copy of the filed court papers via certified mail.

3. Enter into negotiations with your spouse, or your spouse's attorney, regarding the division of all marital property and assets.

4. Have your spouse sign and file a form indicating that he or she agrees to a divorce (often called an AFFIDAVIT OF CONSENT).

5. File a form called a PRAECIPE TO TRANSMIT RECORD with the prothonotary.

Now we shall look at these steps in a little more detail, and later chapters will tell you how to carry out these steps.

Complaint in Divorce. The COMPLAINT IN DIVORCE is a written request for the judge to grant a divorce. A COMPLAINT IN DIVORCE is provided in Appendix C of this book, and full instructions are also provided in later chapters. (see form 4, p.180.) Also included in Appendix C is the COMPLAINT IN DIVORCE used in Philadelphia County. (see form 26, p.209.) Once the COMPLAINT IN DIVORCE is completed, it is taken to the prothonotary to be filed. A filing fee is required that usually ranges between $65 and $120, depending on the county in which you are filing.

Notifying your spouse. After you have prepared the COMPLAINT IN DIVORCE, you need to officially notify your spouse. Even though your spouse may already know that you are filing for divorce, you still need to have him or her officially notified. This is done by having a copy of your COMPLAINT IN DIVORCE delivered to your spouse. This must be done in a certain way, which will be explained in detail later in Chapter 7.

Settlement negotiations. Once all of your paperwork is filed, you need to contact your spouse or your spouse's attorney. This is often done by contacting the party in writing, with a request for a statement of assets, pension plan funds, 401k information, valuable marital property, etc. However, you may already have this information at your fingertips, in which case you may send a letter offering a proposal of property distribution.

This process can be done verbally and less formally, and may even be completed before the COMPLAINT IN DIVORCE is filed. This process opens up a dialogue. This can often be done over the telephone. Child support and custody agreements can be finalized at meetings with court officials. (see Chapter 6.)

Affidavits of Consent. Finally, you have discussed all property matters, and asset distribution and have reached a fair settlement to both parties' satisfaction. You agree as to how your property should be divided, how custody of your children is to be arranged, and how the children are to be supported. If it applies to your situation, there may also be an agreement as to whether alimony will be paid.

If you and your spouse agree on these matters, you will sign an AFFIDAVIT OF CONSENT. (see form 16, p.197.) Your spouse will sign an AFFIDAVIT OF CONSENT. (see form 17, p.198.) The court will approve your agreement.

NOTE: *If you are filing in Philadelphia County, you will use different, but similar, forms. These will be explained in detail in later chapters.*

The judge can order the husband and wife to a *master's hearing* when they are having a difficult time reaching agreement on the major issues. Also, marriage counseling can be ordered if the judge believes the marriage can be saved; however, this is an extremely rare situation. The judge can also direct the state Department of Children and Youth Services to conduct a study and provide the judge with a custody recommendation. Master's Hearings will be addressed later in this book.

Praecipe to Transmit Record. This is your final step in the process. A PRAECIPE TO TRANSMIT RECORD must be filed with the prothonotary. (see form 12, p.191.) Any signed AFFIDAVIT OF CONSENT, MARITAL PROPERTY SETTLEMENT AGREEMENT, RECORD OF DIVORCE OR ANNULMENT, and CERTIFICATE (PROOF) OF SERVICE must also be filed at this time. You now await the judge's review of your paperwork and DECREE OF DIVORCE. (See form 18, p.199 or the decree form required in your county.)

If you cannot locate your spouse, or get a signed AFFIDAVIT OF CONSENT, the procedure will be slightly different and other forms will be needed. (see form 16, p.197 and form 17, p.198.) These differences will be discussed in later chapters of this book.

LEGAL RESEARCH

This book has been designed so that you do not need to do research. However, if you need or want to find out more about the divorce law in Pennsylvania, this section will give you some guidance.

STATUTES

Pennsylvania Divorce Code. The main source of information on Pennsylvania divorce law is the *Pennsylvania Divorce Code*. This is the portion of the law passed by the Pennsylvania Legislature (i.e., the Pennsylvania Statutes) that specifically relates to divorce cases. Selected portions of the Code are found in Appendix A of this book. The complete Code may be found as an individual book that only contains the *Pennsylvania Divorce Code*, or in Title 23 of *Purdon's Pennsylvania Consolidated Statutes Annotated* (which is discussed further below). You can usually find it at the public library, although check to be sure they have the most recent edition. You may also find it at your nearest law library, which is often located in your county courthouse or at a university campus where a law school is located.

PENNSYLVANIA
CONSOLIDATED
STATUTES
ANNOTATED

All of the laws passed by the Pennsylvania Legislature may be found in a set of books titled *Purdon's Pennsylvania Consolidated Statutes Annotated* (Pa. Cons. Stat. Ann). These books contain all of the statutes (not just those relating to divorce cases). Each statute is followed by summaries (called *annotations*) of court cases which discuss and interpret that section of the statutes.

CASES

In addition to the laws passed by the legislature, law is also made by the decisions of the judges in various cases each year. To find this *case law* you will need to go to a law library. Each county has a law library connected with the court, so you can ask the prothonotary where the library is located. Also, law schools have libraries which may be open to the public.

Do not be afraid to ask the librarians for assistance. They cannot give you legal advice, but they can tell you where the books are located. Case law may be found in *Purdon's Pennsylvania Consolidated Statutes Annotated*, as well as in the sources listed below.

Pennsylvania Digest. The *Pennsylvania Digest* is a set of books that gives short summaries of cases, and the place where you can find the court's full written opinion. The digest is arranged alphabetically by subject. Find the chapter on "Divorce," then look for the headings of the subject you want.

Atlantic Reporter. The *Atlantic Reporter* is where the appeals courts publish their written opinions on the cases they hear. There are two *series* of the Atlantic Reporter, the older cases being found in the *Atlantic Reporter* (abbreviated "A."), and newer cases being found in the *Atlantic Reporter 2d Series* ("A.2d"). For example, if the digest gives you a reference to "*Smith v. Smith*, 149 A.2d 721," this tells you that the case titled "Smith v. Smith" can be found by going to Volume 149 of the *Atlantic Reporter 2d Series*, and turning to page 721.

PENNSYLVANIA
RULES OF COURT

The *Pennsylvania Rules of Court* are the rules that are applied in the various courts in Pennsylvania, and they also contain some approved forms. These rules mainly deal with forms and procedures. You would be primarily concerned with the *Rules of Civil Procedure*.

PRACTICE
MANUALS

In addition to the sources mentioned above, you may also find *practice manuals* which are books, or sets of books, covering specific areas of the law. For example, there are practice manuals for drunk driving cases, probate, bankruptcy—and divorce. A divorce practice manual will explain the law, and usually provide sample forms. The law librarians can help you locate such books.

The Internet can be a useful tool to provide both sources and education related to the domestic relations issues associated with a divorce. Searching by key words such as "Pennsylvania Divorce," "Divorce Law," and "Domestic Relations," can provide a host of information and sites (or links) that will assist you in better understanding the process.

LAWYERS 3

Whether you need an attorney will depend upon many factors, such as how comfortable you feel handling the matter yourself, whether your situation is more complicated than usual, and how much opposition you get from your spouse. It may be advisable to hire an attorney if you encounter a judge with a hostile attitude, or if your spouse gets a lawyer who wants to fight. There are no court appointed lawyers in divorce cases, so if you want an attorney, you will have to hire one.

A very general rule is that you should consider hiring an attorney whenever you reach a point where you no longer feel comfortable representing yourself. This point will vary greatly with each person, so there is no easy way to be more definite.

NOTE: *You should hire an attorney if your spouse is in the military, as military divorces are complicated.*

A more appropriate question is: "Do you want a lawyer?" The next section will discuss some of the "pros" and "cons" of hiring a lawyer, and some of the elements you may wish to consider in making this decision.

Deciding if You Want a Lawyer

One of the first questions you will want to consider, and most likely the reason you are reading this book, is: How much will an attorney cost? Attorneys come in all ages, shapes, sizes, sexes, racial, and ethnic groups—and also price ranges. For a very rough estimate, you can expect an attorney to charge anywhere from $250 to $2,000 for an uncontested divorce, and $800 and up for a contested divorce. Lawyers usually charge an hourly rate for contested divorces, ranging from about $75 to $300 per hour. Most new (and therefore less expensive) attorneys would be quite capable of handling a simple divorce, but, if your situation became more complicated, you would probably prefer a more experienced lawyer. As a general rule, you can expect costs to be more than what you think it will cost at the beginning.

Advantages to Hiring a Lawyer

The following are some advantages to hiring a lawyer:

- Judges and other attorneys may take you more seriously. Most judges prefer both parties to have attorneys. They feel this helps the case move in a more orderly fashion because both sides will know the procedures and relevant issues. Persons representing themselves often waste time on matters that have no bearing on the outcome of the case.

- A lawyer will serve as a "buffer" between you and your spouse. This can lead to a quicker passage through the system by reducing the chance for emotions to take control and confuse the issues.

- For the same reasons that are listed above, attorneys prefer to deal with other attorneys. However, if you become familiar with this book, and conduct yourself in a calm and proper manner, you should have no trouble. (Proper courtroom manners are discussed in Chapter 7.)

- You can let your lawyer worry about the details. By having an attorney, you need only become generally familiar with the contents of this book, as it will be your attorney's job to file the proper papers in the correct form, and to deal with the prothonotary, the judge, the process server, your spouse, and your spouse's attorney.

- Lawyers provide professional assistance with problems. In the event your case is complicated, or suddenly becomes complicated, it is an advantage to have an attorney who is familiar with your case. It can also be comforting to have a lawyer to turn to for advice and answers to your questions.

ADVANTAGES TO REPRESENTING YOURSELF

On the other hand, there are also advantages to representing yourself, such as:

- You save the cost of a lawyer.

- Sometimes judges feel more sympathetic toward a person not represented by an attorney. This sometimes results in the unrepresented person being allowed a certain amount of leeway with the procedure rules.

- The procedure may be faster. Two of the most frequent complaints about lawyers received by the bar association involve delay in completing the case and failure to return phone calls. Most lawyers have a heavy caseload, which sometimes results in lapses of time in addressing cases. If you are following the progress of your own case you will be able to push it along the system diligently.

- Selecting an attorney is not easy. As the next section shows, it is hard to know whether you are selecting an attorney with whom you will be happy.

MIDDLE GROUND

You may want to look for an attorney who will be willing to accept an hourly fee to answer your questions and give you help as you need it. This way you will save some legal costs, but still receive some professional assistance. You will also establish a relationship with an attorney who will be somewhat familiar with your case in the event things become complicated and you need a full-time lawyer.

SELECTING A LAWYER

FINDING
LAWYERS

Selecting a lawyer is a two-step process. First, you need to decide with which attorney you will make an appointment, then you need to decide if you wish to hire (retain) that attorney.

Search the Internet. Many attorneys now advertise on the Internet, and attorney referral services operated by a host of private organizations provide names, locations, and specialties of attorneys in your area.

Ask a friend. A common, and frequently the best, way to find a lawyer is to ask someone you know to recommend one to you. This is especially helpful if the lawyer represented your friend in a divorce or other family law matter.

Lawyer referral service. You can find a referral service by looking in the yellow pages phone directory under "Attorney Referral Services" or "Attorneys." This is a service, usually operated by a bar association, that is designed to match a client with an attorney handling cases in the area of law the client needs. The referral service does not guarantee the quality of work, nor the level of experience or ability of the attorney. Finding a lawyer in this manner will at least connect you with one who is interested in divorce and family law matters, and probably has some experience in this area.

Yellow pages. Check under the heading for "Attorneys" in the yellow pages phone directory. Many of the lawyers and law firms will place display ads indicating their areas of practice, and educational backgrounds. Look for firms or lawyers that indicate they practice in areas such as "divorce," "family law," or "domestic relations." Big ads are not necessarily indicative of expertise. Keep in mind that some lawyers do not need to advertise.

Ask another lawyer. If you have used the services of an attorney in the past for some other matter (for example, a real estate closing, traffic ticket, or a will), you may want to call and ask if he or she could refer you to an attorney whose ability in the area of family law is respected.

EVALUATING A
LAWYER

From your search, you should select three to five lawyers worthy of further consideration. Your first step will be to call each attorney's office, explain that you are interested in seeking a divorce, and ask the following questions:

- Does the attorney (or law firm) handle divorces?

- What is the fee range and what is the cost of an initial consultation? (Do not expect to get a definite answer on a divorce fee, but the attorney may be able to give you a range or an hourly rate. You will probably need to meet with the lawyer for anything more detailed.)

- How soon can you get an appointment?

Most offices require you to make an appointment. Once you get in contact with the attorney at the appointment, ask the following questions:

- How much will it cost?

- How will the fee be paid?

- How long has the attorney been in practice?

- How long has the attorney been in practice in Pennsylvania?

- What percentage of the attorney's cases involve divorce cases or other family law matters? (Do not expect an exact answer, but you should get a rough estimate that is at least twenty percent.)

- How long will it take? (Do not expect an exact answer, but the attorney should be able to give you an average range and discuss things that may make a difference.)

If you get acceptable answers to these questions, it is time to ask yourself the following questions about the lawyer:

- Do you feel comfortable talking to the lawyer?

- Is the lawyer friendly toward you?

- Does the lawyer seem confident in himself or herself?

- Does the lawyer seem to be straight-forward with you, and able to explain issues so you understand?

If you get satisfactory answers to all of these questions, you probably have a lawyer with whom you will be able to work. Most clients are happiest if they feel comfortable with their attorney.

WORKING WITH A LAWYER

In general, you will work best with your attorney if you keep an open, honest, and friendly attitude. Also, consider the following suggestions.

ASK QUESTIONS

If you want to know something or if you do not understand something, ask your attorney. If you do not understand the answer, tell your attorney and ask him or her to explain it again. You should not be embarrassed to ask questions. Many people who say they had a bad experience with a lawyer either did not ask enough questions or had a lawyer who would not take the time to explain things to them. If your lawyer is not taking the time to explain what he or she is doing, it may be time to look for a new lawyer.

BE THOROUGH

Give your lawyer complete information. Anything you tell your attorney is confidential. An attorney can lose his license to practice if he or she reveals information without your permission. So do not hold back. Tell your lawyer everything, even if it does not seem important to you. There are many things that seem unimportant to a non-attorney, but can change the outcome of a case. Also, do not hold something back because you are afraid it will hurt your case. It will definitely hurt your case if your lawyer does not find out about it until he or she hears it in court from your spouse's attorney! But if your lawyer knows in advance, he or she can plan to eliminate or reduce damage to your case.

ACCEPT REALITY

Listen to what your lawyer tells you about the law and the system. It will do you no good to argue because the law or the system does not work the way you think it should. For example, if your lawyer tells you that the judge cannot hear your case for two weeks, do not try demanding that he or she set a hearing tomorrow. By refusing to accept reality, you are only setting yourself up for disappointment. And remember: It is not your attorney's fault that the system is not perfect, or that the law does not say what you would like it to say.

PATIENCE

Be patient. This applies both to being patient with the system (which is often slow as we discussed earlier), as well as being patient with your attorney. Do not expect your lawyer to return your phone call within an hour. Your lawyer may not be able to return it the same day. Most lawyers are very busy. It is rare that an attorney can maintain a full caseload and still make each client feel as if he or she is the only client.

THE SECRETARY

Talk to the secretary. Your lawyer's secretary can be a valuable source of information. Be friendly and get to know the secretary. Often he or she will be able to answer your questions, and you will not get a bill for the time you talk to the secretary.

DEALING WITH YOUR SPOUSE

Let your attorney deal with your spouse. It is your lawyer's job to communicate with your spouse, or with your spouse's lawyer. Let your lawyer do his or her job. Many lawyers have had clients lose or damage their cases when the client decides to say or do something on their own.

PROMPTNESS

Be on time. This applies to both appointments with your lawyer and to court hearings.

KEEP YOUR CASE MOVING

Many lawyers operate on the old principle of the squeaking wheel gets the oil. Work on a case tends to be put off until a deadline is near, an emergency develops, or the client calls. There is a reason for this. Many lawyers take more cases than can be effectively handled in order to earn the income they desire. Your task is to become a squeaking wheel that does not squeak too much. Whenever you talk to your lawyer ask the following questions:

- What is the next step?

- When do you expect it to be done?

- When should I talk to you next?

Call your lawyer if you do not hear anything when you expect. Do not remind your lawyer of the missed call; just ask how things are going.

FIRING YOUR LAWYER

If you can no longer work with your lawyer, it is time to either go it alone or get a new attorney. You will need to send your lawyer a letter stating that you no longer desire his or her services and are discharging him or her from your case. Also state that you will be coming by his or her office the following day to pick up your file. The attorney does not have to give you his or her own notes or other work he or she has in progress, but he or she must give you the essential contents of your file (such as copies of papers already filed or prepared and billed for, and any documents that you provided).

If the lawyer refuses to give you your file, for any reason, contact the Pennsylvania Bar about filing a complaint, or *grievance*, against the lawyer. Of course, you will need to settle any remaining fees charged for work that has already been done by the lawyer.

Preliminary Considerations 4

The following things should be done or considered before you begin the divorce process.

Residency

In order to be eligible to file for divorce in Pennsylvania, either you or your spouse must be a resident of Pennsylvania for a period of at least six months immediately before filing.

RESIDENCY VERSUS DOMICILE

It is important to distinguish between the terms *resident* and *domiciliary*. You are a *resident* of a state if you live in that state at least part of the time. You are a *domiciliary* of the state that you consider to be the primary and permanent state in which you live. A person may be a resident of more than one state, but may only be a domiciliary of one state.

Example 1: You live seven months of the year in Florida and five months in Pennsylvania. You consider Florida to be the primary place you live, and use your Florida address for your voter registration, income tax returns, car registration, driver's license, and to receive most of your important mail. You are a domiciliary of Florida, and a resident of both Florida and Pennsylvania. You may file for divorce in Pennsylvania, provided you have been a resident for at least the past six months.

Example 2: Your main home is in Chatsworth, New Jersey; but you also own a townhome in Philadelphia because that is where you work. You typically spend Friday through Sunday in New Jersey and stay in Philadelphia the rest of the week. You consider New Jersey to be the primary place you live, and use your Chatsworth address for your voter registration, income tax returns, car registration, driver's license, and to receive most of your important mail. You are a domiciliary of New Jersey, and a resident of both New Jersey and Pennsylvania. You may file for divorce in Pennsylvania, provided you have been a resident for at least the past six months.

TEMPORARY
ABSENCES

It is not necessary that you or your spouse have been physically in Pennsylvania for the entire six month period before filing, but only that the period of your residency began at least six months ago. For example, during the six month period you may leave Pennsylvania for business, visiting relatives, for a vacation, or to return to the state where you are domiciled; as long as you do not abandon your residence in Pennsylvania.

RESIDENCY
DISPUTES

Generally, residence will only become an issue if your spouse makes it one. There is no conclusive test that can be applied to decide whether a person is, or is not, a resident. In a dispute over residency, the judge will look at all the circumstances and determine whether you or your spouse meets the residency requirement. However, as you will see in the next section of this chapter, if you are clearly a resident of another state, there is little need to try to stretch the definition of residency in order to file in Pennsylvania—you can probably get a divorce more quickly and easily in another state.

WHICH
COUNTY

Your divorce case may be filed in the county where either of you reside. You could also file in any county that you both agree upon, provided the court in that county approves; however, there are few situations in which this would be practical (such as where you both will soon be moving to another county and want to be close to the court that will be handling your case).

GROUNDS FOR DIVORCE

As stated in Chapter 1, there are nine legal bases for divorce available in Pennsylvania. The seven fault grounds would involve complicated proof problems, so we will only discuss the two no-fault provisions in depth.

MUTUAL
CONSENT

If you and your spouse agree that you want a divorce, and will cooperate in filing the necessary papers, you can use the mutual consent provision under Section 3301(c) of the Divorce Code, that your marriage is irretrievably broken and you both agree to a divorce.

LIVING SEPARATE
AND APART

If your spouse is not in agreement, you can use the provision under Section 3301(d) of the Divorce Code, that you and your spouse have lived separate and apart for a period of two years, and your marriage is irretrievably broken.

FAULT GROUNDS
AND OTHER
ALTERNATIVES

If you need to file for divorce now and cannot use either of these no-fault provisions because your spouse will not agree to the divorce and you have not lived separate and apart for the past two years, you have two choices:

1. File now, using one or more of the fault grounds. This may require hiring an attorney because it can get complicated to prove the fault grounds. The fault ground most often used asserts that your spouse has rendered your marital condition or circumstance intolerable, thus making your married life so burdensome that you cannot continue as husband and wife. This ground is known as *indignities*. (Section 3301(a)(6) of the Divorce Code.) Although this sounds like it requires terrible behavior on the part of your spouse, the courts have liberally interpreted this to describe incompatibility, and almost any kind of marital disagreement or problem (e.g., as to lifestyle, spending habits, verbal abuse or use of offensive language, jealousy, differences in religious belief, communication problems, or interference of relatives) can be the basis for a divorce.

2. Move to another state and become a resident there, so that you can file for divorce in that state. Most states have much shorter residency periods than Pennsylvania.

> *Warning:* There are many problems that can arise in this situation, so if you think you may want to do this, you should consult an attorney in Pennsylvania and an attorney in the state where you intend to file for divorce. The information provided here is only for the purpose of making you aware of the possibility of filing in another state and to give you some basic information so that you can better discuss this option with an attorney.
>
> To determine how long it takes to get a divorce, you need to consider the residency requirement, any required separation period, any waiting period required by law, and the backlog of cases the court may have. You also need to be aware of how the laws of that state (regarding property division, child custody and support, alimony, etc.) differ from the laws of Pennsylvania. You may not want a faster divorce if you will be losing an advantage in one or more of these areas.

The following information on a few states will give you an idea of what may be possible. The shortest residency requirements are Alaska (you must be a resident; there is no time limit), Idaho (six weeks), Nevada (six weeks), South Dakota (you must be a resident at the time of filing and continue to be one until the divorce is final; but a hearing may not be held nor a final decree entered until sixty days after filing), and Washington (you must be a resident; there is no time limit; but the decree cannot be entered until ninety days after the spouse is served with papers).

A sixty day residency requirement applies in Kansas and Wyoming.

There is a three month residency requirement in Hawaii and Utah (but the decree cannot be entered until ninety days after filing).

Ninety days as a *domiciliary* is required in Arizona (but the final hearing cannot be held until sixty days after the spouse is served with papers) and Colorado (but the decree cannot be entered until ninety days after the spouse is served).

Six month's residency is required in Alabama, California (but a judgment is not final for six months), Delaware, Florida, Georgia (but a judgment cannot be issued until thirty days after your spouse is served), Indiana (but the final hearing cannot be held until sixty days after filing), Maine, New Mexico, North Dakota (six months before entry of final decree, not before filing), Oregon, and Wisconsin (but a hearing cannot be set until 120 days after the spouse is served). Six months *domicile* is required in Texas (but the decree cannot be entered until sixty days after filing) and Virginia.

The following states have a 180 day residency requirement: Kentucky (but a judgment cannot be entered until the parties have lived apart for sixty days, or until sixty days after the spouse is served if there are children), Michigan (but the final hearing cannot be held until sixty days after filing, or six months after filing if there are any children), and Minnesota.

YOUR SPOUSE

You need to evaluate your situation with respect to your spouse. Have both of you already agreed to get a divorce? If not, what kind of reaction do you expect from your spouse? Your expected reaction can determine how you proceed. If he or she reacts in a rational manner, you can probably use the mutual consent procedure (described in Chapter 8) or the standard uncontested procedure (described in Chapter 9). However, if you expect an extremely emotional and possibly violent reaction, you will need to take steps to protect yourself, your children, and your property; and you will have to start out expecting to employ all necessary court procedures. Be sure to read the section in Chapter 12 on "Protecting Yourself, Your Children, and Your Property."

Unless you and your spouse have already mutually decided to get a divorce, you do not want your spouse to know you are thinking about filing for divorce. This is a defense tactic, although it may not seem that way at first. If your spouse knows or suspects that you are planning a divorce, he or she may take certain steps to prevent you from getting a fair result. These steps include withdrawing money from bank accounts, hiding information about income, and hiding assets. So do not let on until you have collected all of the information you will need and are about to file with the court, or until you are prepared to protect yourself from violence, if necessary.

> *Warning*: Tactics such as withdrawing money from bank accounts and hiding assets raise potential legal action. If you try any of the tactics described above, you risk looking like the bad guy before the judge. This can result in anything from having disputed matters resolved in your spouse's favor, to being ordered to produce the assets (or being jailed for contempt of court).

Theoretically, the system would prefer that you keep evidence of the assets (such as photographs, sales receipts, or bank statements) to present to the judge if your spouse hides them. Then your spouse will be the bad guy and risk being jailed. However, once your spouse has taken assets and hidden them, or sold them and spent the money, even a contempt order may not get the money or assets back.

If you determine that you need to get the assets in order to keep your spouse from hiding or disposing of them, be sure you keep them in a safe place, and make a thorough list of them to be utilized at the appropriate time. The DOMESTIC RELATIONS INCOME AND EXPENSE STATEMENT provides a handy guide for this purpose. (see form 7, p.183.)

Do not dispose of assets. If your spouse claims later that you took them, you can explain to the judge why you were afraid that your spouse would dispose of them and that you merely got them out of his or her reach.

FINANCIAL INFORMATION

It is extremely important that you collect all of the pertinent financial information. This information should include originals or copies of the following:

☐ your most recent income tax return (and your spouse's if you filed separately);

☐ the most recent W-2 tax forms for yourself and your spouse;

☐ any other income reporting papers (such as interest, stock dividends, etc.);

☐ your spouse's most recent paystub, hopefully showing year-to-date earnings (otherwise try to get copies of all paystubs since the beginning of the year);

☐ deeds to all real estate; and titles to cars, boats, or other vehicles;

☐ your and your spouse's will;

☐ life insurance policies;

☐ stocks, bonds, or other investment papers;

☐ pension or retirement fund papers and statements;

☐ health insurance card and papers;

☐ bank account or credit union statements;

☐ your spouse's social security number, and driver's license number;

☐ names, addresses, and phone numbers of your spouse's employer, close friends, and family members;

☐ credit card statements, mortgage documents, and other credit and debt papers;

☐ a list of vehicles, furniture, appliances, tools, etc., owned by you and your spouse (see the next section in this chapter on "Property and Debts" for forms and a detailed discussion of what to include);

☐ copies of bills or receipts for recurring, regular expenses, such as electric, gas or other utilities, car insurance, etc;

☐ copies of bills, receipts, insurance forms, or medical records for any unusual medical expenses (including for recurring or continuous medical conditions) for yourself, your spouse or your children; and,

☐ any other papers showing what you and your spouse earn, own, or owe.

Make copies of as many of these papers as possible, and keep them in a safe and private place (where your spouse will not find them). Try to make copies of new papers as they come in, especially as you get close to filing court papers.

NEGOTIATION

It is important to remember that many key aspects to receiving exactly what you desire in a divorce center upon effective negotiation. Your MARITAL PROPERTY SETTLEMENT AGREEMENT can be crafted (and later entered as an order of court) in any fashion you choose, providing of course that your spouse agrees to the settlement proposal. (see form 9, p.185.) Keep in mind, the better your skill at presenting the proposal to your spouse, the better your chances that he or she will accept it with little or no change. The more favorable that you make your spouse's offer appear, the more likely it is that he or she will not entirely object to your terms. Negotiation is both a skill and an art. If you feel as though you could not attempt to undertake this process, you should consider consulting with an attorney. Negotiating will be addressed more fully in Chapter 7.

Property, Debts, and Alimony 5

This chapter will explain how property and debts are divided, when alimony is awarded, and if it is, how the amount and duration of alimony are determined. These subjects are grouped together here because there is some relationship between them, and they must be considered in any divorce, regardless of whether you and your spouse have any children. (The issues of child custody, visitation, and support will be discussed in Chapter 6.)

By applying the information in this chapter to your situation, you will get an idea of what to expect if the judge must decide these matters. If you and your spouse are trying to come to an agreement on these matters, this chapter will help you to decide what proposal to offer or accept.

Property

This section is designed to give you an idea of the manner in which the division of property occurs in a divorce and to prepare you for completing some of the court papers you will need to file. It will also guide you in completing the PROPERTY INVENTORY. (see form 1, p.177.) This form is a list of all of your property and key information about that property. Some of what applies to property also applies to debts, so there will be some mention of debts in this section.

MARITAL AND
NONMARITAL
PROPERTY

First, you will need to understand how property is divided into *marital* and *nonmarital* property. Trying to determine how to divide assets and debts can be difficult. Under Pennsylvania's *equitable distribution* law, assets and debts are separated into two categories: marital (meaning it is both yours and your spouse's), and nonmarital (meaning it is yours or your spouse's alone). In making this distinction the following rules apply:

- If the asset (or debt) was acquired after the date you were married, it is presumed to be a marital asset or debt. It is up to you or your spouse to prove otherwise.

- A nonmarital asset (or debt) is one that was acquired before the date of your marriage. It is also a nonmarital asset if you acquired it through a gift or inheritance (as long as it was not a gift from your spouse). Income from nonmarital property is also nonmarital property (for example: rent you receive from an investment property you had before you got married). If you exchange one of these assets or debts after your marriage, it is still nonmarital.

  Example: You had a $6,000 car before you were married. After the marriage, you traded it for a different $6,000 car. The new car is still nonmarital property.

  Also, items acquired after you and your spouse have separated are nonmarital property. Finally, you and your spouse may sign a written agreement that certain assets and debts are to be considered nonmarital or marital.

- Marital assets and debts are those acquired during your marriage, even if they were acquired by you or your spouse individually. This includes the increase in value of a nonmarital asset during the marriage or is due to the use of marital funds to pay for or improve the property. All rights accrued during the marriage in pension, retirement, profit-sharing, insurance, and similar plans are marital assets. It is also possible for one spouse to make a gift of nonmarital property to the other spouse, thereby making it marital property.

- Real estate that is in both names is considered marital property, and it is the responsibility of the spouse claiming otherwise to prove it.

- Finally, whether an asset or debt is marital or nonmarital, and the value of any asset, is determined as of the date of a settlement agreement, or the date the COMPLAINT IN DIVORCE was filed, whichever is first.

PROPERTY
INVENTORY

The PROPERTY INVENTORY calls for a specific, detailed listing of your property. (see form 1, p.177.) The PROPERTY INVENTORY is divided into six columns, designated as follows:

☛ **N.** The "N" stands for *nonmarital*. Place an "H" in this column to designate any items you believe to be the husband's nonmarital property, and a "W" to designate any items you believe to be the wife's nonmarital property. Leave this column blank for any items that are marital property.

☛ **Amount.** This is the value of the item at the time the item was purchased or received.

☛ **Property.** Give a general description and the location of the item.

☛ **Assigned to Whom.** Indicate whether you or your spouse will keep the item.

☛ **Misc. Info.** In this section, you can state any important fact regarding the property.

☛ **Current Value.** This is the current market value of the item.

Use these five columns to list your property, including the following:

Cash. For each account, list the name of the bank, credit union, etc., and the account number. This includes savings and checking accounts and certificates of deposit ("CDs"). The balance of each account should be listed in the columns. Make copies of the most recent bank statements for each account.

Stocks and bonds. All stocks, bonds, or other "paper investments" should be listed. Write down the number of shares and the name of the company or other organization that issued them. Also, copy any notation such as "common" or "preferred" stock or shares. This information can be obtained from the stock certificate itself, or from a statement from the stock broker. Make a copy of the certificate or the statement.

Real estate. List each piece of property you and your spouse own. The description might include a street address for the property, a subdivision name and lot number, or anything that lets you know to which piece of property you are referring. There probably will not be an ID number, although you might use the county's tax number. Real estate (or any other property) may be in both of your names (*joint*), in your spouse's name alone, or in your name alone. The only way to know for sure is to look at the deed to the property. (If you cannot find a copy of the deed, try to find mortgage papers or payment coupons, homeowners insurance papers, or a property tax assessment notice.) The owners of property are usually referred to on the deed as the *grantees*.

In assigning a value to the property, consider the market value, which is the amount for which you will probably sell the property. You could consider the amount for which similar houses in your neighborhood have sold. You may also consider how much you paid for the property. *Do not* use the tax assessment value, as this is usually considerably lower than the market value.

Vehicles. This category includes cars, trucks, motor homes, recreational vehicles ("RVs"), motorcycles, boats, trailers, airplanes, and any other means of transportation for which the State requires a title and registration. Your description should include the following information (which can usually be found on the title or on the vehicle itself):

- year it was made.

- make: The name of the manufacturer, such as "Ford," "Honda," "Chris Craft," etc.

- model: You know it is a Ford, but is it a Mustang, an LTD, or an Aerostar: The model may be a name, a number, a series of letters, or a combination of these.

- serial number: This is most likely found on the vehicle, as well as on the title or registration.

Make a copy of the title or registration. For a value, go to the public library and ask for the *blue book* for cars, trucks, or whatever vehicle you have. A blue book (which may be yellow, black, or any other color) gives the average values for used vehicles. Your librarian can help you find what you need. Another source is the classified advertising section of a newspaper which helps you to find selling prices for vehicles. You might also try calling a dealer to see if he can give you a rough idea of the value. Be sure you take into consideration the condition of the vehicle.

Furniture. List furniture as specifically as possible. Include the type (such as sofa, coffee table, etc.), the color, and, if you know it, the manufacturer, line name, or style. Furniture usually does not have a serial number, although if you find one be sure to write it on the list. Just estimate a value, unless you just know what it is worth.

Appliances, electronic equipment, and yard machines. This category includes such items as refrigerators, lawn mowers, and power tools. Again, estimate a value, unless you are familiar enough with them to know what they are worth. There are too many different makes, models, accessories, and age factors to be able to figure out a value otherwise. These items will probably have a make, model, and serial number on them. You may have to look on the back, bottom, or other hidden place for the serial number, but try to find it.

Jewelry and other valuables. You do not need to list inexpensive costume jewelry. You can plan on keeping your own personal watches, rings, etc. However, if you own an expensive piece you should include it on your list, along with an estimated value. Be sure to include silverware, original art, gold, coin collections, antiques, etc. Again, be as detailed and specific as possible.

Life insurance with cash surrender value. This is any life insurance policy that you may cash in or borrow against, and therefore has value. If you cannot find a cash surrender value in the papers you have, you can call the insurance company and ask for the information.

Other "big ticket" items. This is simply a general reference to anything of significant value that does not fit into one of the categories already discussed. Examples might be a portable spa, an above-ground swimming pool, golf clubs, guns, pool tables, camping or fishing equipment, farm animals, or machinery.

Pensions. The division of pensions and retirement benefits can be complicated. Whenever these types of benefits are involved and you cannot agree on how to divide them, you will need to consult an attorney or a CPA to determine the value of the benefits and how they should be divided. Be sure to read the section in Chapter 12 on "Pension Plans."

What not to list. You will not need to list your clothing and other personal effects. Pots, pans, dishes, and cooking utensils ordinarily do not need to be listed, unless they have some unusually high value.

DIVIDING
PROPERTY

Once you have completed your list, go back through it and try to determine who should end up with each item. The ideal situation is for both you and your spouse to go through the list together, and divide the items fairly. However, if this is not possible, you will need to create a reasonable settlement proposal to submit to your spouse or your spouse's attorney. Consider each item, and make a check mark to designate whether that item should go to the husband or wife. You may make the following assumptions.

- Your nonmarital property will go to you.

- Your spouse's nonmarital property will go to your spouse.

- You should get the items that only you use.

- Your spouse should get the items only used by your spouse.

- The remaining items should be divided, evening out the total value of all the marital property, and taking into consideration who would really want that item.

To somewhat equally divide your property (we are only talking about marital property here), you first need to know the total value of your property. First of all, do not count the value of the nonmarital items. Add the remaining amounts, which will give you an approximate value of all marital property.

When it comes time for your initial settlement proposal, you and your spouse may be arguing over some or all of the items on your list. This is when you will be glad that you made copies of the documents relating to the property on your list. Arguments over the value of property may need to be resolved by hiring appraisers to set a value; however, you will have to pay the appraiser a fee. Dividing your property will be discussed further in later chapters.

DEBTS

This section relates to the DEBT INVENTORY, which will list your debts. (see form 2, p.178.) Although there are many cases where, for example, the wife gets a car but the husband is ordered to make the payments, generally whoever gets the property also gets the debt owed on that property. This seems to be a fair arrangement in most cases. On form 2, you will list each debt owed by you or your spouse. As with nonmarital property, there is also nonmarital debt. This is any debt incurred before you were married that is yours alone. You will be responsible for your nonmarital debts, and your spouse will be responsible for his or her nonmarital debts.

> ***Warning:*** If you and your spouse are jointly responsible for a debt, you are not relieved of your obligation to pay just because your spouse agrees to pay (or is ordered to pay) the debt in the divorce proceeding. If your spouse does not pay, the creditor can still pursue you for payment. You would then need to take your spouse to court to get him or her to reimburse you.

DEBT INVENTORY

The **DEBT INVENTORY** calls for a specific, detailed listing of your debts. (see form 2, p.178.) The **DEBT INVENTORY** is divided into six columns, designated as follows:

☞ **N.** The "N" stands for *nonmarital*. Place an "H" in this column to designate any debt you believe to be the husband's nonmarital debt, and a "W" to designate any debt you believe to be the wife's nonmarital debt. Leave this column blank for any items that are marital debts.

☞ **Amount.** This is the amount of the debt at the time it was incurred.

☞ **Debt.** State what the debt was incurred for, such as "car," "vacation," "dining set," etc. Be as specific as necessary to clearly identify the debt.

☞ **Assigned to Whom.** Indicate whether you or your spouse will be responsible for paying the debt.

☞ **Misc. Info.** Give any important fact regarding the debt, such as who purchased the item and why.

☞ **Current Balance.** This is the balance currently owed.

ALIMONY

Generally, over the past decade, Pennsylvania courts have been moving away from court-ordered alimony payments. The underlying theory is that the alimony payment creates an ongoing link of one spouse to the other. The court hopes to eliminate the necessity of such spousal interaction. Despite this fact, alimony is still utilized in many cases.

TYPES OF
ALIMONY

Alimony may be granted to either the husband or the wife. In reality, there are few cases in which a wife will be ordered to pay alimony to her husband. There are two types of alimony:

1. *Rehabilitative.* This is for a limited period of time and is to enable one of the spouses to get the education or training necessary to find a job. This is usually awarded when one of the parties has not been working during the marriage.

2. *Permanent.* This continues for a long period of time, possibly until the death of the party receiving the alimony. This is typically awarded when one of the parties is unable to work due to age or a physical or mental illness.

ALIMONY FACTORS

The alimony statute requires the judge to consider several factors when making a determination on a request for alimony. (Pennsylvania Consolidated Statutes Annotated (Pa. Cons. Stat. Ann.), Title (Tit.) 23, Section (Sec.) 3701.) These are used both to determine whether alimony should be awarded and, if so, how much to award and for how long. The factors are:

- the relative earnings and earning capacities of the parties;

- each party's age and physical, mental, and emotional condition;

- each party's sources of income including medical, retirement, and insurance benefits;

- each party's "expectations and inheritances;"

- the duration of the marriage;

- any contribution of one party to the other party's education, training, or increased earning power;

- the extent to which either party's earning power, expenses, or financial obligations are affected by serving as a custodian of the parties' children;

- the standard of living established during the marriage;

- the parties' relative education, and the time needed to acquire education and training to become adequately employed;

- the parties' relative assets and liabilities;

- the property brought into the marriage;

- either party's contribution as a homemaker;

- the relative needs of the parties;

● any marital misconduct during the marriage up to the date of separation;

● any tax ramifications;

● whether the party seeking alimony lacks sufficient property to provide for his or her needs; and,

● whether the party seeking alimony is incapable of self-support through employment.

As an alternative to requesting alimony, you may want to try to negotiate to receive a greater percentage of the property instead. This may be less of a hassle in the long run, but it may also change the tax consequences of your divorce. See the section in Chapter 12 on "Taxes."

CHILD CUSTODY, VISITATION, AND SUPPORT 6

This chapter will explain how child custody, visitation, and support issues are determined. By applying the information in this chapter to your situation, you will get an idea of what to expect if the judge must decide these matters. If you and your spouse are trying to reach an agreement on these matters, this chapter will help you to decide whether a proposal is reasonable.

CHILD CUSTODY AND VISITATION

The decision to live apart is a difficult one for anyone; however, it is most painful when children are involved in the family separation. Children have no part in the parents' determination to live separately. However, when parents do split, it has enormous effect upon their young lives. Children feel torn, questioning the proper way in which to show affection to both parents when they are no longer together as a family. Despite the end of a couple's relationship, a mother and father have an undeniable responsibility and duty to continue to care for and make decisions that directly affect their children. The parents' choice in these decisions ultimately will manifest itself through the children's behavior, stability, and confidence in himself or herself. Although the couple's relationship may terminate, both the mother and father will continue to be parents.

CUSTODY
CONCILIATION
OFFICE

The central focus of the Custody Conciliation Office as it exists in its capacity as an arm of the Domestic Relations Section is to aid parents in structuring certain terms of their shared custody arrangement through effectuating a binding legal document. The Custody Office in your area provides a non-threatening, non-adversarial mediation session in which both parties are encouraged to negotiate and communicate their goals for parenting (such as structured partial custody times with each parent) through the assistance of a neutral third party Conciliator.

The process of Custody Conciliation involves varying levels of parental communication. Several steps in the custody process are put in place to provide parents with every opportunity to fashion an arrangement to which they may be firmly committed. It is obvious that a schedule that you develop on your own, and not one that is imposed upon you by the Court, will be one that you will more comfortably find acceptable. Thus, the purpose of the Custody Conciliators and the goal of the Custody Conferences is not to assess who may be the better parent but rather to assist in preserving and maintaining the indispensable bond and relationship your children are entitled to experience with both parents.

The first step in the Custody Conciliation process involves both parents attending a four-hour seminar entitled "Children Cope with Divorce" or some similar titled program. Certain of the program's objectives include examining the experience of separation and divorce from the children's perspective, exchanging certain skills which parents may utilize to support the children's adjustment to the separation, and discussions that involve the manner by which to avoid placing children in a no-win situation with parents. Generally, there is a small cost for the program and your attendance is mandatory if either of you are involved in a divorce or custody proceeding.

CONSENT
CUSTODY ORDER
BY AGREEMENT

If the fortuitous circumstance presents itself such that both parents are in agreement regarding their shared custody arrangements, and they wish to have that agreement formalized into an Order of Court, both parents must appear voluntarily for a Custody Conference. Both parents must also have attended the four-hour "Children Cope with

Divorce" above-mentioned. At this conference level, the Conciliator puts into writing all of the terms to which you as the parties agree and provides to you the required documentation to obtain a Docket Number to have your agreement entered as a Court Order. There is a filing fee for this process and you should check with your Domestic Relations Section for the cost in your area.

Even though both parents may have verbally agreed to certain custody arrangements, and both have been functioning without these arrangements previously being reduced to writing, it is highly recommended that you seek a formal Order of Court. The Order of Court will serve as a fall back document, or a guide, whenever potential disagreements as to custody arrangements may occur...and they will.

FILING A CUSTODY COMPLAINT

Should no agreement exist as to the terms of your custody arrangement, or if either party refuses to meet at a voluntary Custody Conciliation Conference, then you must proceed by petitioning the Court for a Custody Order. A Court Petition takes the form of a Complaint. As is the case with all custody situations, each party must appear at an Intake Conference and each must attend the "Children Cope with Divorce" seminar. The forms for filing a Custody Complaint are affixed on page 182 of this book. Should you not wish to file your own Complaint, an attorney may prepare and file one on your behalf.

THE CUSTODY INTAKE CONFERENCE

A Custody Intake Conference will be scheduled once you have completed the "Children Cope with Divorce" seminar. The conference is an informal session, not a Hearing and no evidence or testimony is formally presented. The children are not to be present nor are they interviewed. There is no third party (for example a friend of the family or a grandparent) to be present in the conference. Although it is not necessary for your attorney to be present during a Custody Conference, it is recommended that you seriously discuss with your counsel potential benefit of having him or her present to represent you at the conference.

Custody Orders are as different and varied as are individuals. Each Order is crafted and developed based upon an examination of each couple's circumstance. You are the best person to make the determination as to the needs of your children and your lifestyles. The Custody Conference provides a forum for you to present information about what is best for you and your children. It is not the Court's goal to interfere or dictate personal decisions unless compelled to do so because the parties are ultimately unable to fashion a workable custody arrangement. Thus, at the Custody Conciliation Conference, areas of agreement and disagreement are highlighted and the parties have the opportunity to smooth out points of contention and fashion an arrangement for custody with the assistance of the Custody Conciliation Supervisor.

Once the terms of your agreement are reduced to writing, they will be formalized into an Order of Court and signed by the Family Court Judge. Truly, most matters are resolved at this level. However, if complete agreement on the custody terms cannot be reached at this stage, you will then be scheduled to attend a Conciliation Conference. In the meantime, a Temporary Order of Court will be put in place and you must obey that Order until the second conference. The goal of the Temporary Order of Court is to make certain that no breach in contact or communication between the children and both parents occurs until such time that a more permanent arrangement can be finalized.

CUSTODY
CONCILIATION
CONFERENCE

The goal of the Custody Conciliation Conference is to encourage agreement between the parties in such manner that both will be committed to a custody arrangement which will be formalized as a Court Order. The Conciliator will assist the parties in reaching an agreement utilizing skills and methods employed in mediation. This conference, as was the last Intake Session, is also informal. There are no records of this proceeding and no evidence or testimony is permitted to be presented. Once again, although it is not necessary for your attorney to be present during a Custody Conference, it is recommended that you seriously discuss with your counsel potential benefit of having him or her present at the conference to represent you.

The Custody Conciliation Conference may take several hours in an effort to resolve the issues and to fashion the terms of your Custody Agreement. If no agreement is reached, the Custody Conciliator will issue a Recommended Order and forward it to the Court for the Judge's signature. You must follow this order.

If you object to the Recommended Order, you must file a Request for an Adversarial Hearing within ten (10) days from the date of the Order. Your matter then will be scheduled for a Trial before the Family Court Judge. You will be notified of the trial date and also of the date of a Pre-Trial Conference which you, or your attorney on your behalf, must attend prior to the scheduled Trial.

The court will usually go along with any custody and visitation arrangement you and your spouse can agree upon, as long as your agreement does not appear to the judge to be detrimental to the child. Most of this section will discuss how custody and visitation decisions will be made when you and your spouse cannot reach an agreement.

THE CUSTODY
OFFICE

When there are minor children, you and your spouse will need to go through the court's *custody office*. The job of the custody office is either 1) assist you in formalizing your custody agreement, if you have one; 2) try to help you reach an agreement; or, 3) make a recommendation to the judge about custody if no agreement can be reached.

Custody Process Guidance

QUESTION: Are you and your spouse in agreement in regards to the shared custody of your child (children)?

YES — 1. Call the custody office for an appointment.

2. Attend an *intake conference* (the first meeting with the custody officer).

3. Attend the "Children Coping With Divorce" seminar. This is an informative, and required, seminar addressing the needs and concerns of children who are caught in the divorce process.

NO — 1. File a petition.

2. Attend the Children Coping With Divorce seminar.

3. Attend an intake conference.

QUESTION: Did an agreement result from the intake conference?

YES — No further action is necessary. You will receive a copy of the handwritten agreement at the end of the intake conference. In a week to ten days you will receive your court order.

NO — A temporary order will be issued and a *custody conference* will be scheduled.

QUESTION: Did the custody conference result in an agreement?

YES — No further action is necessary. You will receive a copy of the handwritten agreement at the end of the custody conference. In a week to ten days you will receive your court order.

NO — The conciliator will prepare a recommended order and forward it to the court. You must follow this order unless or until it is changed by another court order.

QUESTION: Do you agree with the recommended order?

YES — No further action is necessary. In a week to ten days you will receive the court order.

NO — If you object to the recommended order, you may file a Request for Adversarial Hearing within ten days from the date you receive the recommended order in the mail. You may telephone the custody office to obtain a Request for Adversarial Hearing form. Each county has its own requirements, and there is a fee, usually about $50. The adversarial hearing will be before a judge.

CUSTODY
PRINCIPLES

Generally, if you are the wife, the odds start out in favor of you getting custody. But do not depend upon the odds. Start out by reviewing the guidelines the judge will use to decide the custody question. These can be found on page 57. For each item listed in that section, write down an explanation of how that item applies to you. This will be your argument when you have your hearing with the judge.

Child custody tends to be something that cannot be negotiated. It is more often used as a threat by one of the parties in order to get something else, such as more of the property or lower child support. If the real issue is one of these other matters, do not be concerned by a threat of a custody fight. In these cases, the other party probably does not really want custody and will not fight for it. If the real issue is - custody, you will not be able to negotiate for it and will end up letting the judge decide anyway.

Many custody battles revolve around the *moral fitness* of one or both of the parents. If you become involved in this type of a custody fight, you should consult a lawyer. Charges of moral unfitness (such as illegal drug use, child abuse, or immoral sexual conduct) can require long court hearings involving the testimony of many witnesses, as well as possibly the employment of private investigators. For such a hearing, you will require the help of an attorney who knows the law, the right questions to ask witnesses, and the rules of evidence.

However, if the only question is whether you or your spouse have been the main caretaker of the child, you can always have friends, neighbors, and relatives come into the hearing (if they are willing to help you out) to testify on your behalf, and it may not be necessary for you to have an attorney. But if you need to subpoena unwilling witnesses to testify, you should have an attorney.

As with everything else in a divorce, situations are ideal when both parties can agree on the question of custody of the children. Generally, the judge will accept any agreement you reach, provided it does not appear that your agreement will cause harm to your children. With respect to child custody, the Pennsylvania law makes it clear that the primary interest of the court is to protect and provide for the *best interests* of the child.

It is the official public policy of Pennsylvania to assure that each minor child has frequent and continuing contact with both parents after the parents separate or the marriage of the parties is dissolved, and to encourage parents to share the rights and responsibilities of child rearing. After considering all relevant facts, the father of the child will be given the same consideration as the mother in determining the primary residence of a child, irrespective of the age or sex of the child.

In spite of this modern philosophy voiced by Pennsylvania (and many other states), you may find that many judges believe that (all things being equal) a young child is better off with the mother. Because of these statements in the law, a judge may go to great lengths to find that all things are not equal, thus justifying a decision to award custody to the mother. This occurs frequently throughout many states and the Commonwealth of Pennsylvania, and it is a reality you may have to face. To be fair, however, more cases than ever before show fathers being awarded significant custodial rights.

The practice in Pennsylvania law is for the court to order that the parental responsibility for a minor child be shared by both parents, unless the court finds that shared parental responsibility would be detrimental to the child. This indicates that, in most cases, the court favors what is commonly known as *shared custody* or *joint custody*. However, very few parents can put aside their anger at each other to agree on what is best for their child. Shared custody may lead to more fighting. If shared custody is ordered, the child may still have a primary residence. In many cases in which custody is equally shared, no primary residence is required except for the purpose of school information.

CUSTODY FACTORS

If you and your spouse cannot agree upon how these matters will be handled, you will be leaving this important decision up to the judge. The judge cannot possibly know your child as well as you and your spouse, so it makes sense for you to work this out yourselves.

If the judge must decide the question, he or she will consider the following factors:

- which parent is most likely to encourage and allow frequent and continuing contact with the other parent;

  NOTE: *The Pennsylvania custody statute requires the judge to consider this factor. (Pa. Cons. Stat. Ann., Title 23, Section 5301.) Although the following factors are not set forth in the custody statute, applicable case law requires the judge to consider them when making a custody decision.*

- the love, affection, and other emotional ties existing between the child and each parent;

- the ability and willingness of each parent to provide the child with food, clothing, medical care, and other material needs;

- the length of time the child has lived with either parent in a stable environment;

- the permanence, as a family unit, of the proposed custodial home;

- the moral fitness of each parent;

- the mental and physical health of each parent;

- the home, school, and community record of the child;

- the age of the child or special needs of the child, and which parent is most able to attend to those needs; or,

- any other fact the judge decides is relevant.

It is difficult to predict the outcome of a custody battle. There are too many factors and individual circumstances to make such a guess. The only exception is where one parent is clearly unfit and the other can prove it. The most common charges against a spouse are drug abuse or physical or sexual abuse. However, unless there has been an arrest and conviction, it is difficult to prove. In general, do not charge your spouse with being unfit unless you can prove it. Judges are not impressed with unfounded allegations, and such charges often do more harm than good.

If your children are older (not infants), it may be a good idea to seriously consider their preference for with whom they would like to live. Your fairness and respect for their wishes may benefit you in the long run. Just be sure that you keep in close contact with them and visit them often. Knowing their preference may assist you in voicing your position, but keep in mind that a child's preference generally is not considered by Pennsylvania courts in making custody determinations.

CHILD SUPPORT

As you have by now gathered through your review and reading of this book, Pennsylvania's Common Pleas Courts have jurisdiction over matters of family law such as divorce, property division, alimony, child custody, paternity, protection from abuse (PFA), as well as child and spousal support. While most of these cases originate in the Prothonotary's Office, child and spousal support matters are handled through the Domestic Relations Section of the Common Pleas Court. Support, whether child or spousal, is determined by a set of established guidelines that the Supreme Court of the Commonwealth of Pennsylvania created.

Each of the Commonwealth's sixty-seven counties has a Domestic Relations Section. You may locate the Domestic Relations Section of the Common Pleas Court in your area by looking in the blue pages of your local telephone book.

In Pennsylvania, as in most states, the question of child support is mostly a matter of a mathematical calculation. Getting a fair child support amount depends upon the accuracy of the income information presented to the court. If you feel fairly sure that the information your spouse presents is accurate, or that you have obtained accurate information about his or her income, there is not much to debate. The court will simply take the income information provided, use the formula to calculate the amount, and order that amount to be paid.

In most cases, there will not be much room to argue about the amount of child support, so there usually is not a need to get an attorney. If you claim your spouse has not provided accurate income information, this may be the time to consult an attorney, who will know how to obtain more accurate income information. Your attorney (or you) may set up a support conference before a *support counselor* at your county courthouse. A support counselor reviews your income along with your spouse's income to determine the amount of support.

If child support is involved in your case, you should first work out what you think the court will order based upon the child support guidelines discussed below. Do this before discussing the matter with your spouse. If you will be receiving child support, you may want to ask for more than the guidelines require, and negotiate down to what the guidelines suggest.

If you will be paying child support, you may want to try for slightly less than the guidelines call for, but keep in mind that the support counselor will probably look at the schedule and ask questions if you and your spouse are agreeing to less. This does not mean the support counselor will reject your agreement, but you may need to offer an explanation as to why you are not following the guidelines.

You can tell your spouse that there is little room for negotiation on child support as the court will probably require it be set according to the statute. If your spouse will not agree to something very close to the guidelines, give up trying to work it out and let the support counselor decide.

Pennsylvania law establishes the legal duty to provide financial support for children and spouses. Once again, the master will probably agree with any arrangement you and your spouse reach, as long as he or she is satisfied that the child will be taken care of adequately. The following information and the DOMESTIC RELATIONS INCOME AND EXPENSE STATEMENT will give you an idea of your financial base regarding child support. (see form 7, p.183.)

NOTE: *You may also hear attorneys, judges, and other court personnel refer to form 7 as a* Child Support Income and Expense Questionnaire *or a* Financial Affidavit.

Make a copy of the SUPPORT GUIDELINE COMPUTATIONS—CHILD SUPPORT to use as a worksheet to get a rough idea of your income and expenses. (see form 8, p.184.) Later, as you prepare form 8 for filing, you will refer back to this section for instructions on completing the form.

HOW CHILD
SUPPORT IS
DETERMINED

When an agreement cannot be reached, the following procedure will be used. Generally, there are two factors used to determine the amount of support to be paid:

1. the needs of the child and

2. the financial ability of each parent to meet those needs. Pennsylvania has simplified this procedure by establishing a formula to be used in calculating both the needs of the child and each parent's ability to meet those needs. In filling out the SUPPORT GUIDELINE COMPUTATIONS—CHILD SUPPORT, be sure to convert everything to monthly amounts. (see form 8, p.184.) The following instructions are used in determining the proper amount of support:

☞ First, fill in the top of form 8 with the county at the top, docket number (from the prothonotary), names of the parties, date, and county.

☞ Determine each party's average monthly gross income. This is usually done by taking the gross income for the past six months and dividing by six. Gross income includes:

- wages, salary, fees, and commissions;

- net income from business or dealings in property;

- interest, rents, royalties, and dividends;

- pensions and all forms of retirement;

- income from an interest in an estate or trust;

- alimony paid to you;

- social security benefits, temporary and permanent disability benefits, workmen's compensation, and unemployment compensation;

- capability of income is considered when a party willfully fails to obtain appropriate employment (age, education, work experience, etc., are considered in determining earning capacity);

- bonuses, may be annualized and considered carefully, particularly in times of economic difficulty; and

- income from seasonal employment, which will ordinarily be based upon a yearly average.

Write the gross income per pay period for both parents on line 1.

☞ Determine each party's net income. Net income is determined by taking the gross income, and subtracting the following items:

- federal, state, and local income taxes;

- FICA payments;

- non-voluntary retirement payments;

- union dues;

- health insurance premiums for the benefit of the other party or the child(ren); and,

- alimony paid to the other party.

Write the net income per pay period for both parents on line 2.

☞ If you have not already done so, convert your income to a monthly figure and put that net amount on line 3 for both parents.

☞ Add the incomes of both parents and write that amount on line 4.

☞ Apply the child support guidelines. The example of form 8 on page 184 is based upon support of a wife and one minor child. The defendant earns $1,053 per month *net* (i.e., after allowed deductions are subtracted from gross income). The plaintiff earns $725 per month net. Find the appropriate percentage on the Chart of Proportional Expenditures on page 66, and write that percentage on line 5.

☞ Follow the self-explanatory mathematical formula on form 8 at line 6.

Example: For one minor child, with combined incomes of $1,778, the percentage is twenty percent (which will be .20 in the mathematical calculation). The defendant's obligation would be $209.80 per month for one child, and $35.46 per month for spousal support, for a total of $246.26 per month for a wife and one minor child.

NOTE: *The chart on page 66 is the chart in effect at the time this book went to press. Since this chart can change at any time, you should obtain the most current chart from the prothonotary, the court's support office, or a law library.*

☞ Determine if there are special circumstances that justify a further adjustment. In deciding whether to deviate from the amount of support determined by the guidelines, the judge will consider:

- unusual needs and unusual fixed obligations;

- other support obligations of the parties;

- other income in the household;

- ages of the children;

- assets of the parties;

- medical expenses not covered by insurance;

- standard of living of the parties and their children; and

- other relevant and appropriate factors, including the best interests of the child.

NOTE: *Failure to deviate from the guidelines by considering a party's actual expenditures where there are special needs and special circumstances is a misapplication of the guidelines.*

The deviation applies to the amount of the support obligation, not to the amount of income. The court may apply a ten percent deviation up or down depending upon certain circumstances. Write this additional support on line 7.

☞ Add lines 6 and 7 together and put the total on line 8. This is the total support.

☞ Divide each parent's line 3 (monthly amount) by line 4 and write each parent's percent value on line 9.

☞ Multiply line 8 by each parent's percentage in line 9 (do not forget that percentages are changed to decimals—59% is .59.) Write each value for each parent. See page 65 for an example. This is what each parent pays in child support.

☞ Write the values in line 3 (monthly amount) in line 11 and 12. Make sure you put the proper parent's values in those lines (defendant and plaintiff parents).

☞ Subtract line 12 from line 11 and write that amount at line 13.

☞ Write the defendant parent's value from line 10 at line 14.

☞ Subtract line 14 from line 13. Write this amount in line 15.

☞ Line 16 says to multiply line 15 by 30% (.30). Write this amount on line 17. This is the amount of spousal support.

☞ Add line 17 and the defendant's line 10 and put this value on line 18 for a total support award.

☞ If there are no dependent children, fill out lines 19-23.

☞ Write line 3 values in 19 and 20, subtract line 20 from line 19, and write this amount at line 21.

☞ Multiply line 21 by 40% (.40) and write this value at line 23.

CHILD SUPPORT AGENCIES

There are two agencies you need to be aware of:

Central collection office. The "collections office" is the agency that processes the child support and alimony payments. This is frequently a division of the support office. The spouse responsible to pay the support (or his or her employer) will make payments to the depository. The collection's office then cashes that check and issues a check to the spouse entitled to receive support or alimony.

Child Support Enforcement office. The Child Support Enforcement office is responsible for enforcing the payment of child support to parents receiving support and others who request their services. If you are to receive support and you would like to use the enforcement services of this office you will need to contact your local Child Support Enforcement office. This may not be necessary if your spouse goes on an income deduction order immediately and keeps his or her job. But if some payments are missed, you may call the Child Support Enforcement office at any time and ask for their assistance. Income deduction is mandatory in Pennsylvania.

_____ **COUNTY**

D.R.S.

Docket _____   Date _____

Defendant _____   C.O. _____

Plaintiff _____

Rule 1910.16-3 Support Guidelines Formula

(a) The formula for the determination of the amount of support is as follows:

SUPPORT GUIDELINE COMPUTATIONS

CHILD SUPPORT

		DEFENDANT	PLAINTIFF
1.	Total Gross Income Per Pay Period	8,775.00	6,041.00
2.	Net Income	6,318.00	4,350.00
3.	Conversion to Monthly Amount	1,053.00	725.00
4.	COMBINE INCOME OF BOTH DEFENDANT AND PLAINTIFF		1,778.00
5.	Proportionate Expenditure (determined from chart)		x .20 %
6.	Basic Child Support (multiply #4 by #5)		= 355.60
7.	Additional support if required		
8.	Total Support		355.60
9.	Percentage of each parent's obligation (divide line #3 by #4)	59 %	41 %
10.	Each parent's obligation	$ 209.80	$ 145.80

SPOUSAL SUPPORT WITH DEPENDENT CHILDREN

11.	DEFENDANT'S MONTHLY NET INCOME	$ 1,053.00
12.	LESS PLAINTIFF'S MONTHLY NET INCOME	- $ 725.00
13.	DIFFERENCE	$ 328.00
14.	LESS DEFENDANT'S CHILD SUPPORT OBLIGATION	- $ 209.80
15	DIFFERENCE	$ 118.20
16.	MULTIPLY BY 30%	.30
17.	AMOUNT OF MONTHLY SPOUSAL SUPPORT	$ 35.46
18.	COMBINE SPOUSAL SUPPORT (line 17) AND CHILD SUPPORT FOR A TOTAL SUPPORT AWARD.	

SPOUSAL SUPPORT WITHOUT DEPENDENT CHILDREN

19.	DEFENDANT'S MONTHLY NET INCOME (line #3)	$ _____
20.	LESS PLAINTIFF'S MONTHLY INCOME (line #3)	- $ _____
21.	DIFFERENCE	$ _____
22.	MULTIPLY BY 40%	x _____ .40
23.	AMOUNT OF MONTHLY SPOUSAL SUPPORT	$ _____

RULE 1910.16-3 DRS 10/92

CHART OF PROPORTIONAL EXPENDITURES

The chart of proportional expenditures is as follows:

PROPORTION OF NET MONTHLY INCOME ON CHILDREN BY INCOME LEVEL

Income Levels

Children	$500-$700	$701-$995	$996-$1,143	$1,144-$1,291	$1,292-$1,439
1	23.5	23.0	22.5	22.0	21.5
2	36.5	35.8	35.1	34.4	33.7
3	45.7	44.8	43.9	43.0	42.1
4 or more	50.0	49.0	48.1	47.2	46.3

	$1,440-$1,587	$1,588-$1,735	$1,736-$1,883	$1,884-$2,031	$2,032-$2,179
1	21.0	20.5	(20.0)	19.5	19.0
2	33.0	32.3	31.6	30.9	30.2
3	41.2	40.3	39.4	38.5	37.6
4 or more	45.4	44.5	43.6	42.7	41.8

	$2,180-$2,327	$2,328-$2,475	$2,476-$2,623	$2,624-$2,771	$2,772-$2,919
1	18.5	18.0	17.5	17.0	16.5
2	29.5	28.8	28.1	27.4	26.7
3	36.7	35.8	34.9	34.0	33.1
4 or more	40.9	40.0	39.1	38.2	37.3

	$2,920-$3,067	$3,068-$3,215	$3,216-$3,363	$3,364-$4,000	$4,001-$5,000
1	16.0	15.5	15.0	14.5	14.0
2	26.0	25.3	24.6	23.9	23.2
3	32.2	31.3	30.4	29.5	28.6
4 or more	36.4	35.5	34.6	33.7	32.8

	$5,001-$6,000	$6,001-$7,000	$7,001-$8,000	$8,001-$9,000	$9,001-$10,000
1	13.5	13.0	12.5	12.0	11.5
2	22.5	21.8	21.1	20.4	19.7
3	27.7	26.8	25.9	25.0	24.1
4 or more	31.9	31.0	30.1	29.2	28.3

GENERAL PROCEDURES 7

As a lay person filing your own legal forms, it is critical to understand what is required of you by the court when filing your own divorce. Certain forms are essential to initiate and proceed with your case. This chapter will provide necessary information as to the forms required in pursuing your divorce and how you must complete them.

AN INTRODUCTION TO LEGAL FORMS

Most of the forms in Appendix C of this book follow forms created and officially approved by either the Pennsylvania Supreme Court or by the Philadelphia County Family Court. These forms have one advantage—the prothonotary and judges are not likely to object to them. The forms in this book are legally correct, however one occasionally encounters a troublesome prothonotary or judge who is very particular about how he or she wants the forms drafted. If you encounter any problem with the forms in this book being accepted by the prothonotary or judge, you can try one or more of the following:

- Ask the prothonotary or judge what is wrong with your form, then try to change it to suit the prothonotary or judge.

- Ask the prothonotary or judge if there is a Pennsylvania Supreme Court form (or a county-specific form) available. If there is, find out where you can get it. Then get it and use it. The instructions in this book will still help you to fill it out.

- Consult a lawyer.

Special Note on Philadelphia Forms

If you will be filing your divorce case in Philadelphia County, you will find that the court there is very particular about how things must be done and has its own required forms. In Appendix C you will find some forms that are required in Philadelphia. When the authors requested forms from the Philadelphia family court clerk's office, we received many forms of very poor quality.

Some of these forms also contain errors, such as one that refers to grounds for divorce as a "Three (2) Year Separation Where the Court Determines That There is a Reasonable Prospect of Reconciliation." The correct grounds are a *two* year separation where the court finds there is *no* reasonable prospect of reconciliation. Therefore, we recreated these forms in much better quality for Appendix C. However, there is no guarantee that the Philadelphia family court clerk will accept the forms from Appendix C, and you may find that you need to obtain the forms from the Philadelphia family court clerk's office.

Although the instructions in this book will tell you to "type in" certain information, it is not absolutely necessary to use a typewriter. If typing is not possible, you can *print* the information required in the forms as long as it can be easily read. Otherwise the prothonotary's office may not accept your papers for filing.

Warning: Some, if not all, of the counties require the use of black ink. If you write the information instead of typing, be sure to use a pen with black ink. However, when you *sign* any form, use blue ink. Never use red, green, or any other unusual ink color.

Each form is referred to by both the title of the form and a form number. Be sure to check the form name and number because some of the forms have similar sounding names. Also, a list of the forms, by name, is found at the beginning of Appendix C. You will notice that most of the forms in Appendix C have similar headings that identify the court, the parties, and the case number.

The top portion of these court forms will all be completed as follows:

☛ Fill in the name of the county in which you will file your papers.

☛ Fill in the case number. There may also be a division designation that is to indicate which judge is assigned to your case. The case number and division will be assigned when you file your COMPLAINT IN DIVORCE and any other initial papers with the prothonotary. The prothonotary will write in the case number and division on your COMPLAINT IN DIVORCE and any other initial papers. You will fill in the number and division on any papers you file at a later date.

☛ Fill in your full name on the line marked "Petitioner" or "Plaintiff," and your spouse's full name on the line marked "Respondent" or "Defendant." Do not use nicknames or shortened versions of names. You should use the names as they appear on your marriage license, if possible.

When completed, the top portion of your forms should look something like the following example:

IN THE COURT OF COMMON PLEAS OF_____ERIE_____COUNTY, PENNSYLVANIA

RHETT BUTLER_____,

          Plaintiff,

                                    Case No.:____10537-1997____

  V.

                                    Division:____FAMILY____

SCARLETT O'HARA BUTLER_____,

          Defendant.

At the end of many of the forms there will be a place for you to sign your name, and type in your name, address, and phone number. You will also notice that your signature must be notarized on certain forms, in which case a provision is included on the form for completion by the notary public.

FILING WITH THE PROTHONOTARY

Once you decide which forms you need, and have them all prepared, it is time to file your case with the prothonotary. First, make at least three copies of each form (the original for the prothonotary, one copy for yourself, one for your spouse, and one extra just in case the prothonotary asks for two copies or you decide to hire an attorney later).

Filing is about as simple as making a bank deposit, although the following information will help the process go smoothly. Call the prothonotary's office. (You can find the phone number under the county government section of your phone directory.) Ask the following questions (along with any other questions that come to mind, such as where the prothonotary's office is located and their hours):

- How much is the filing fee for a COMPLAINT IN DIVORCE?

- Does the court have any special forms that need to be filed with the complaint? If there are special forms that do not appear in this book you will need to go down to the prothonotary's office and pick them up. There may be a fee, so ask.

- How many copies of the petition and other forms do you need to file with the prothonotary?

Next, take your COMPLAINT IN DIVORCE, and any other forms you determine you need to the prothonotary's office. (Instructions for completing these forms are provided in other parts of this book.) The prothonotary handles many different types of cases, so be sure to look for signs telling you which office or window to go to. You should be looking for signs that say such things as "Family Court," "Family Division," "Filing," etc. If it is too confusing, ask someone where you file a **Complaint in Divorce**.

Once you have found the right place, simply hand the papers to the prothonotary and say, "I'd like to file this." The prothonotary will examine the papers, then do one of two things: either accept it for filing (and either collect the filing fee or direct you where to go to pay it), or tell you that something is not correct.

If you are told something is wrong, ask the prothonotary to explain to you what is wrong and how to correct the problem. Although prothonotaries are not permitted to give legal advice, the types of problems they spot are usually very minor things that they can tell you how to correct. Often it is possible to figure out how to correct it from the way they explain what is wrong.

Notifying Your Spouse

A basic sense of fairness (in addition to the laws of Pennsylvania) requires that a person be notified of a legal proceeding that involves him or her. In all cases, you are required to notify your spouse that you have filed for divorce. This gives your spouse a chance to respond to your **Complaint in Divorce**. (see form 4, p.180.)

If you are unable to find your spouse (and therefore cannot have him or her served by certified mail-return receipt requested) you may choose to have him or her personally served by the sheriff. If your spouse cannot be found, see the subsection entitled "If You Cannot Find Your Spouse," on page 112. The notice requirements as they relate to your particular situation will be discussed in later chapters.

Notice of Filing the Complaint

Certified Service. The usual way to notify your spouse that you filed for a divorce is called *certified service*, which is done by mail. Certified service involves mailing your documents by "certified mail, return receipt requested." A green card is attached to the envelope containing copies of your **COMPLAINT IN DIVORCE**. Your spouse will have to sign this card in order to get the envelope from the mailman or post office. The signed card is then returned to you, which will appropriately document your mailing and your spouse's receipt of the papers. There is a minimal fee for this service (usually about $2 in addition to the postage).

Personal Service. Instead of using certified service, you can have the sheriff, or someone else designated by the judge, personally deliver the papers to your spouse (this is called *personal service*). If your spouse refuses to accept certified mail, you will need to use personal service, which entails a fee, usually about $20. Call the sheriff's office in the county where your spouse lives and ask how much it will cost to have him or her served with divorce papers, and what forms of payment they accept (they may not accept personal checks).

Deliver two copies of your **COMPLAINT IN DIVORCE**, together with the attached cover sheet and affidavits you filed and a check or money order for the service fee to the sheriff's office. A sheriff's deputy will personally deliver the papers to your spouse. Of course, you must give the sheriff accurate information about where your spouse can be found.

To do this, fill out a sheriff's instructions form, which can be obtained from your local sheriff's office. This form will have places for you to fill in addresses and other information that will assist the sheriff in locating and serving your spouse. If there are several addresses where your spouse might be found (such as a friend's or relative's house) list them, along with any other information that may help the sheriff find your spouse (such as the hours your spouse works).

The deputy will fill out a form to verify that the papers were delivered (including the date and time they were delivered), and will file a copy of that form with the prothonotary and return another copy to you.

OTHER NOTICES Once your spouse has been served with the **COMPLAINT IN DIVORCE**, you may simply mail him or her copies of any papers you file later. All you need to do is sign a statement (called a *Certificate of Service*) verifying that you mailed copies to your spouse. Some of the forms in this book will include a certificate of service section for you to complete. If any form you file does not contain one you will need to complete the CERTIFICATE (PROOF) OF SERVICE. (see form 11, p.190.) The form is rather clear about what information is to be filled in. On the line after the phrase: "I Certify That The," type in the title of what you are sending, such as "Petition for Temporary Custody." Form 11 is to be filed with the prothonotary as proof that you sent a copy.

SETTING A HEARING

If you should set a hearing date for any child support, spousal support, or child custody matters you will need to notify your spouse. Setting the date for a support hearing simply requires that you go to the support office and request a hearing date and time. The support officer will have you complete certain paperwork, and you will later receive a notice of the date and time of the hearing. Once you know your hearing date and time, you must send a notice to your spouse. This is done by preparing a NOTICE OF HEARING. (see form 19, p.200.)

- ☛ Fill in the top of the form according to the instructions on page 69.

- ☛ Type in your spouse's name and address (or his or her attorney's name and address) on the lines after the word "TO:."

- ☛ Fill in all of the blanks on the form for the court or judge's name, date, time, and location of the hearing (including the name and address of the courthouse).

- ☛ On the line after the phrase "on the following matter:" type in the kind of hearing, such as "Motion for Support or Custody."

Make three copies of the NOTICE OF HEARING and mail one copy to your spouse. File the original with the custody office and keep two copies for yourself.

COURTROOM MANNERS

There are certain rules of procedure that are used in a court. These are essentially rules of good conduct, or good manners, and are designed to keep the proceedings orderly. Many of the rules are written down, although some are unwritten customs that have developed over many years.

They are not difficult, and most of them make sense. Following these suggestions will make the judge respect you for your maturity and professional manner, and possibly even make him or her forget for a moment that you are not a lawyer. It will also increase the likelihood that you will receive the things you request.

RESPECT

Show respect for the judge or master. This basically means do not do anything to make the judge or master angry at you, such as arguing with him or her. Be polite, and call the judge or master "Your Honor" when you speak to him or her, such as "Yes, Your Honor," or "Your Honor, I brought proof of my income." (If the master wishes to be called by his or her name, or by another title, he or she will let you know.) Although many lawyers address judges as "Judge," this is not proper.

You should wear appropriate clothing (coat and tie for men and a dress or suit for women). Do not wear T-shirts, blue jeans, shorts, or "revealing" clothing. Many of the following rules also relate to showing respect for the court.

COURTESY

Anytime the judge or master is talking, you need to be listening carefully. Even if the master interrupts you, stop talking immediately and listen. Masters can become upset if you do not allow them to interrupt.

ONE AT A TIME

Each person is allotted his or her own time to talk in court. The master can only listen to one person at a time, so do not interrupt your spouse when it is his or her turn. As difficult as it may be, stop talking if your spouse interrupts you. (Let the master tell your spouse to keep quiet and let you have your say.)

TALK TO THE
MASTER

Many couples get in front of a master and begin arguing with each other. They turn away from the master, face each other, and begin arguing as if they are in the room alone. Usually, this has several negative results: The master cannot understand what either one is saying since they both start talking at once, they both look like fools for losing control, and the master gets angry with both of them.

Whenever you speak in a courtroom, look only at the master. Try to pretend that your spouse is not there. Remember, you are there to convince the master that you should have certain things. You do not need to convince your spouse.

WAIT YOUR
TURN

The usual procedure is for you to present your case first. When you are done saying all you came to say, your spouse will have a chance to say whatever he or she came to say. Let your spouse have his or her say. When he or she is finished you will have another chance to respond to what has been said.

STICK TO THE
SUBJECT

Many people tend to get off track and start telling the master all the problems with their marriage over the past twenty years. This wastes time and aggravates the master. Stick to the subject, and answer the master's questions simply and to the point.

KEEP CALM

Masters like things to go smoothly in their hearing rooms. They do not like shouting, name calling, crying, or other displays of emotion. Generally, masters do not like family law cases because they get too emotionally charged. So give your master a pleasant surprise by keeping calm and focusing on the issues.

RESPECT YOUR
SPOUSE

Even if you do not respect your spouse, act like you do. All you have to do is refer to your spouse as "Mr. Smith" or "Ms. Smith" (using his or her correct name, of course).

NEGOTIATING

It is beyond the scope and ability of this book to fully present a course in negotiation techniques. However, a few basic rules may be of some help.

ASK FOR MORE

Asking for more than you want always gives you some room to compromise by giving up a few things. You may end up with close to what you really want. With property division, this means you will review your **PROPERTY INVENTORY** (see form 1, p.177), and decide

- which items you really want;

- which ones you would like to have; and

- which ones you do not care much about.

Also try to figure out which items your spouse really wants, would like to have, and does not care much about. At the beginning you will say that you want certain things. Your list will include:

- everything you really want;

- almost everything you would like to have;

- some of the things you do not care about; and,

- some of the things you think your spouse really wants or would like to have.

Once you find out what is on your spouse's list, you begin trading items. Generally you try to give your spouse things that he or she really wants and that you do not care about, in return for your spouse giving you the items you really care about and would like to have.

Be sure to also look at your **DEBT INVENTORY** and consider what may be owed on each item and who should be responsible for the debt. (see form 2, p.178.) For example, it may be to your advantage (after considering your income and expected expenses after the divorce) to take the older car that is paid off, rather than the newer car with a large payment.

Make a list of what each of you should end up with, using the categories listed above. You will eventually end up with a list of things you can probably get with little difficulty (you really want and your spouse does not care), those that you will fight over (you both really want), and those that need to be divided but can probably be easily divided equally (you both do not really care).

Regarding child support or alimony, ask for more than you really want (or less than you are willing to pay, if you will be paying). Hopefully your spouse will make a counter-offer that is close to what you would prefer. Use the child support calculations you did earlier to get an idea of what the court would probably order, then ask for a bit more (or a bit less if you will be paying support). Just understand that the court will probably order an amount close to what the child support guidelines call for, so there will not be too much room for negotiation.

LET YOUR SPOUSE START

The first person to mention a dollar figure loses. Whether it is a child support figure or the value of a piece of property, try to get your spouse to name the amount he or she thinks it should be first. If your spouse starts with a figure almost what you had in mind, it will be much easier to get to your figure. If your spouse begins with a figure far from yours, you know how far in the other direction to begin your bid.

GIVE YOUR SPOUSE TIME

Your spouse is probably just as afraid as you are about the possibility of losing to the support counselor's or custody conciliator's decision, and would like to settle. Do not be afraid to state your "final offer," then walk away. Give your spouse a day or two to think it over. Maybe he or she will call back and make a better offer. If not, you can always reconsider and make a different offer in a few days, but do not be too willing to do this or your spouse may think you will give in even more.

KNOW YOUR BOTTOM LINE

Before you begin negotiating you should try to set a point that you will not go beyond. If you have decided that there are four items of property that you absolutely must have, and your spouse is only willing to agree to let you have three, it is time to end the bargaining session and go home.

REMEMBER

By the time you have read this far you should be aware of two things:

1. Your property will be divided in a roughly equal portion.
2. The support counselor or judge will probably come close to the child support guidelines.

This awareness should give you an approximate idea of how things will turn out if the judge is asked to decide these issues in a master's hearing or on specific appeal. This should help you to set your bottom line on such matters.

IF YOU CANNOT AGREE

If you are unable to agree on one or more matters, see Chapters 10 and 11 for more information on dealing with a contested case.

A FEW MORE NEGOTIATING TIPS

When one bargains or negotiates, one must simultaneously assert one's self and compromise. Not only can pitiable negotiating talents undermine confidence, on a very practical level they can create a substantial dimple in your pocketbook. According to experts, the following psychological stumbling blocks typically interfere with effective negotiation. Learn to avoid them, and not only will you steal the deal, you will boost your self-esteem and develop a greater sense of control—all important and essential goals in obtaining the result you are seeking in your divorce.

POWER

Many men and women feel uncomfortable with blatant displays of power. Usually, these people have been the "power behind the scenes," so exerting power publicly can be fear-provoking. To deal with—and rise above—that fear, learn to recognize the difference between *positive* and *negative* power. Positive power allows you to protect your interests and fulfill your needs; negative power is used to manipulate and control others. An example of positive power is brushing up on the spousal support requirements and refusing—gracefully, of course—to accept an offer that shortchanges you when you are certain you can do better.

ASSERTIVENESS
VERSUS AGGRESSION

Even in these enlightened days when women are CEOs and cabinet members, many still have apprehensions about being labeled "pushy." Women are frequently afraid to request what they want since they tend to confuse assertiveness with aggression. Many men too, are concerned that they will appear impolite if they are perceived as confrontational. *Aggression* implies violation. When one conducts oneself aggressively, the other person will likely feel angry or disadvantaged. *Assertiveness*, on the contrary, means pursuing what you want without overtly demeaning or intimidating your opponent.

EMPATHY
VERSUS SYMPATHY

When you are empathetic, you feel *with* someone, as opposed to having sympathy, which is feeling *for* someone. While sympathy has its place at a sick friend's bedside, it is not the emotion you want with you at the bargaining table. For example, if you are asking for spousal support and your ex appeals to you with how hard he or she is working, acknowledge that you are aware of the work he or she has done (assuming that to be true), thus showing empathy. Then out-line three reasons why, despite his or her hard work, your support is well-deserved.

DISCOMFORT

One key attribute most women share is the ability to make people feel comfortable. However, if negotiations start getting wobbly, this can become a liability. Should both sides be grasping relentlessly to what they want, women sometimes submit rather than face the discomfort of a clash or impasse. To become comfortable feeling uncomfortable, out-line exactly what you want from the deal, be it a higher alimony amount or an extra day of custody time, and make a note of why you think it is reasonable (you actually can write it out before a confrontation, hearing, or meeting and make a mental list of your arguments). If a contentious moment crops up, recalling those points can aid you in setting aside emotion and solidifying your focus upon the case at hand.

SILENCE

Once both parties have stated their positions, a stretch of silence can hover. Women and men often break the tension by speaking and thus breaking the silence—most likely by settling for a substandard offer. A more effectual strategy is staying tight-lipped. Silence is an essential negotiating tool—the last person to speak throws the ball back into the other's court. Of course, sitting and saying nothing does become awkward. To drive away anxiety, draw a deep breath, relax your facial muscles, and soften your eyes so that you do not glower at your opponent.

MATURITY   Out of nervousness or discomfort, some people often sprinkle their speech with adolescent phrases ("like," "you know" and "do you think?") all of which compromise their authority. Thus, too, does *upspeak*, the habit of raising the pitch of your voice at the end of a sentence, so that even pointed assertions sound like questions. Upspeak is passive, as though the speaker is looking for validation. Practice speaking assertively by dropping your voice before you enter any negotiation.

YOUR GOAL   Think of negotiating as a game. In order to play it, you have to ask for items, entities, or certain outcomes, and sometimes that means asking for what you do not necessarily expect to get. Women tend to ask only for what they really want, while men usually leave wiggle room. The next time you are confronted with a negotiation, be primed to make requests that are several marks above that with which you would be satisfied.

MUTUAL CONSENT DIVORCE 8

There are two ways that a case can be considered *uncontested*. One is where you and your spouse agree to everything from the beginning, and the other is where you and your spouse negotiate or argue, but eventually reach an agreement.

Most lawyers have had the following experience: A new client comes in and says she wants to file for divorce. She has discussed it with her husband, and it will be a "simple, uncontested" divorce. Once the papers are filed, the husband and wife begin arguing over a few items of property. The lawyer then spends a lot of time negotiating with the husband. After much arguing, an agreement is finally reached. The case will proceed in the court as "uncontested," but only after a lot of "contesting" out of court.

For the purposes of this book, an uncontested case is where you will do your arguing and deciding *before* you go to court, and the judge will only be approving your decision. A *contested* case is where you and your spouse will be doing your arguing *in* court, and leaving the decision to the master.

USING THE MUTUAL CONSENT PROCEDURE

You may not know if you are going to have a contested case until you try the uncontested route and fail. Therefore the following sections, and Chapter 9, are presented mostly to assist you in attempting the uncontested case. Chapter 10 specifically discusses the contested case.

BASIC
REQUIREMENTS

In certain circumstances, you may take advantage of Pennsylvania's ninety-day mutual consent divorce procedure. In order to proceed in this fashion, you must meet the following four basic requirements:

1. You or your spouse have resided in Pennsylvania for at least the past six months.

2. You and your spouse do not have any *minor* or *dependent* children; OR you and your spouse agree about who will have custody and the child support terms, so that there will be no need for a hearing on these matters. (A *minor* child is one who is under the age of eighteen. A *dependent* child may be over the age of eighteen, but is still dependent upon you for support due to mental or physical illness, disease, or disability.)

3. You and your spouse have agreed as to how your property and debts will be divided.

4. You will sign an AFFIDAVIT OF CONSENT (see form 16, p.197) and your spouse will sign an AFFIDAVIT OF CONSENT (see form 17, p.198) (other equivalent forms that may be required in your county).

If you meet these four requirements, the mutual consent procedure can be completed in as little as ninety-one days after filing. However, even if you do not meet all four of these conditions, you should still read this chapter as it will help you understand the other procedures better. If the only requirement you do not meet is that you cannot agree on the division of your property, you may want to reconsider your position on the property.

Read this chapter and have your spouse read it, then compare this simple procedure to the procedures in Chapter 9 and Chapter 10 of this book. Once you see how much easier it is when you have an agreement, you may want to try harder to resolve your differences.

NECESSARY FORMS

To begin your divorce case (except in Philadelphia County, which is explained below), the following forms will be filed with the prothonotary's office (see Chapter 7 for filing instructions):

☐ CIVIL COVER SHEET (form 13)

☐ NOTICE TO DEFEND AND CLAIM RIGHTS (form 3)

☐ COMPLAINT IN DIVORCE (form 4)

☐ AFFIDAVIT (form 5), stapled to COMPLAINT IN DIVORCE

☐ COURT OF COMMON PLEAS INTAKE (form 6)

☐ DOMESTIC RELATIONS INCOME AND EXPENSE STATEMENT (form 7)

☐ NOTICE TO FILE SOCIAL SECURITY NUMBERS (form 23)

The following forms will be filed at the conclusion of the ninety days:

☐ MARITAL PROPERTY SETTLEMENT AGREEMENT (form 9)

☐ ACKNOWLEDGMENT (form 10) signed by you, and stapled to the MARITAL PROPERTY SETTLEMENT AGREEMENT

☐ ACKNOWLEDGMENT (form 10) signed by your spouse, and stapled to the MARITAL PROPERTY SETTLEMENT AGREEMENT

☐ AFFIDAVIT OF CONSENT/CONSENT WAIVER (form 16) signed by you

☐ AFFIDAVIT OF CONSENT/CONSENT WAIVER (form 17) signed by your spouse

☐ SUPPORT GUIDELINE COMPUTATIONS—CHILD SUPPORT (form 8), if you have minor children

☐ PRAECIPE TO TRANSMIT RECORD (form 12)

☐ DECREE OF DIVORCE (form 18)

☐ RECORD OF DIVORCE OR ANNULMENT (form 20), commonly called the "vital statistics form"

☐ NOTICE OF INTENTION TO RETAKE PRIOR NAME (form 24), if you are the wife and desire to resume using a former name.

NOTE: *To help you keep track of your case, the preceding list of forms is reproduced as Checklist 1 in Appendix B.*

PHILADELPHIA
COUNTY FORMS

As we have mentioned before, Philadelphia County has its own forms. Although forms 25 through 36 in Appendix C are recreated from the Philadelphia County forms, you may still need to obtain these forms from the Family Court Clerk. Even if you are able to use the forms in Appendix C, you will still need to obtain the Decree forms from the Family Court Clerk.

If you are filing in Philadelphia County, you will file these forms to begin your case:

☐ DOMESTIC RELATIONS INFORMATION SHEET (form 25)

☐ COMPLAINT IN DIVORCE (form 26)

When you are ready to complete your case in Philadelphia County, you will file these forms:

☐ MARITAL PROPERTY SETTLEMENT AGREEMENT (form 33)

☐ ACKNOWLEDGMENT (form 10, or a similar form if you are required to use one obtained from the clerk) signed by you, and stapled to your MARITAL PROPERTY SETTLEMENT AGREEMENT

☐ ACKNOWLEDGMENT (form 10, or a similar form if you are required to use one obtained from the clerk) signed by your spouse, and stapled to your MARITAL PROPERTY SETTLEMENT AGREEMENT

☐ WAIVER OF NOTICE OF INTENTION TO REQUEST ENTRY OF DIVORCE UNDER SEC. 3301(C) OF THE DIVORCE CODE (form 30), signed by you

☐ NOTICE OF INTENTION TO REQUEST ENTRY OF § 3301(C) DIVORCE DECREE (form 31) [if your spouse is *not* represented by an attorney]; or NOTICE OF INTENTION TO REQUEST ENTRY OF DIVORCE (CASES UNDER SECTION 3301(C) OF THE DIVORCE CODE) (form 32) [if your spouse *is* represented by an attorney], signed by you.

☐ PRAECIPE TO TRANSMIT RECORD (form 27)

☐ Decree (obtain form from the Family Court Clerk)

☐ **RECORD OF DIVORCE OR ANNULMENT** (form 20), commonly called the "vital statistics form"

NOTE: *To help you keep track of your case, the preceding list of forms is reproduced as Checklist 2 in Appendix B.*

BASIC PROCEDURE

Basically, the procedure is as follows:

1. You complete and file the necessary forms and serve them upon your spouse.

2. You and your spouse discuss and resolve all property distribution (and child custody and support if applicable).

3. You sign an **AFFIDAVIT OF CONSENT** (form 16), and your spouse signs an **AFFIDAVIT OF CONSENT** (form 17), or equivalent forms that may be required in your county.

4. You file other appropriate forms with the prothonotary in order to complete the case.

5. You wait for your **DECREE OF DIVORCE** to arrive in the mail. There is a waiting period of ninety days after you file your initial papers.

The following is a discussion of the forms used in the mutual consent procedure, and the procedure itself. You will also be referred back to these instructions by later chapters if you need to use the standard or contested procedures.

CIVIL COVER SHEET

You will need to prepare the **CIVIL COVER SHEET**. (see form 13, p.192.) File it along with a **COMPLAINT IN DIVORCE**. (see form 4, p.180.)

NOTE: *The CIVIL COVER SHEET is not used in Philadelphia County.*

To complete the **CIVIL COVER SHEET** (form 13):

☞ Type or print your name on the line marked "Plaintiffs," and your spouse's name on the line marked "Defendants." The prothonotary will fill in the docket number at the time you file your papers.

☞ Items II through VII have already been completed for you.

☞ If there are any other cases that have already been filed and are related to your divorce case (such as a domestic violence case, custody case, etc.), you will need to complete the section under the heading "VIII. Related Case(s) if any." If there are any such cases, fill in the name of the judge, the docket number, and the case case caption (this is the names of the parties as they appear on the court papers in the other case).

☞ Fill in the date on the line marked "Date," and sign your name on the line marked "Signature of Filing Party or Attorney of Record."

DOMESTIC RELATIONS INFORMATION SHEET

If you are filing in Philadelphia County, you will need to file a **DOMESTIC RELATIONS INFORMATION SHEET**. (see form 25, p.207.) This form is self-explanatory; each box on the form clearly indicates what information needs to be filled in there. If you have more than five children, make another copy of the second page of the form and staple it to the other sheet.

NOTICE TO DEFEND AND CLAIM RIGHTS

You must complete a **NOTICE TO DEFEND AND CLAIM RIGHTS**. (see form 3, p.179.) File it along with your **CIVIL COVER SHEET** (see form 13, p.192) and **COMPLAINT IN DIVORCE**. (see form 4, p.180.)

NOTE: *In Philadelphia County, the NOTICE TO DEFEND AND CLAIM RIGHTS has been made the first page of the COMPLAINT IN DIVORCE (see form 26, p.209); therefore, you will not need to complete form 3 if you are filing in Philadelphia County.*

To complete the NOTICE TO DEFEND AND CLAIM RIGHTS (form 3):

☞ Complete the top portion of the form according to the instructions in Chapter 7 on page 69.

☞ On the line in the second paragraph, type in the name of the county where you will file for divorce.

☞ On the lines below the words "Lawyers Referral Service," type in the address and telephone number of the lawyer referral service in the county where you will file for divorce.

☞ Sign your name on the line above the words "For Petitioner," and type in your address and telephone number on the lines as indicated on the form.

COMPLAINT IN DIVORCE

The COMPLAINT IN DIVORCE is the primary paper used to open your case and ask for a divorce. (see form 4, p.180.) This form will be filed along with the CIVIL COVER SHEET (see form 13, p.192), and the NOTICE TO DEFEND AND CLAIM RIGHTS. (see form 3, p.179.) (In Philadelphia, you just use form 26, p.209.)

To complete the COMPLAINT IN DIVORCE (form 4):

☞ Complete the top portion of the form according to the instructions in Chapter 7, page 69.

☞ Type in your name on the line in the first, unnumbered paragraph.

☞ In paragraph 1, type in your name on the first line, and your address on the second line.

☞ In paragraph 2, type in your spouse's name on the first line, and his or her address on the second line.

☞ In paragraph 4, type in the date you were married on the first line, and the state in which you were married on the second line.

☞ In paragraph 5, type in the number of children you and your spouse have (including any adopted children), and their names and birthdates. If there are no children, type in "0" and leave the name and birthdate sections blank.

☞ In paragraph 8, type your name on the line.

☞ ***Do not*** sign yet! Below the signature line, type in your name, address, and phone number on the designated lines. You will sign this form before a notary public, along with other forms.

PHILADELPHIA
COUNTY FORM

If you are filing in Philadelphia County, instead of using form 4, you will need to complete the **COMPLAINT IN DIVORCE.** (see form 26, p.209.) Complete it as follows:

☞ Complete the top portion of the form according to the instructions in Chapter 7.

☞ Under the heading "Notice to Defend and Claim Rights," check the box for "Divorce," as well as the box for each of the of the matters that are included in your divorce case.

Example: If you do not have an attorney you would not check the box for "Attorney Fees." If you are not seeking alimony you would not check the boxes for "Temporary Alimony" and "Alimony." If you do not have any minor children you would not check the boxes for "Support" and "Custody and Visitation."

NOTE: ***Do not*** *check the box for "Annulment of Marriage."*

☞ At the bottom of the first page, check the appropriate boxes to indicate whether there was a former domestic relations case, and whether any of your children are receiving public assistance.

☞ On the second page of form 26, in the first sentence cross out the words "by (his/her) attorney(s)," since you do not have an attorney. (If you do have an attorney, your attorney should be preparing this form for you.)

☞ In paragraph 1, fill in your name, address, and the date you began living at that address in the appropriate spaces.

☞ In paragraph 2, fill in the same information for your spouse.

☞ If both you and your spouse meet the residency requirement, you may leave paragraph 3 as it is. If only you meet the residency requirement, at the end of paragraph 3 add the following: "Only the Plaintiff has been a resident of the Commonwealth of Pennsylvania for the required period of six months." If only your spouse meets the residency requirement, at the end of paragraph 3 add: "Only the Defendant has been a resident of the Commonwealth of Pennsylvania for the required period of six months."

☞ In paragraph 4, in the appropriate spaces, fill in the date you were married and the state in which you were married.

☞ In the space in paragraph 5, type in: "The marriage of the parties is irretrievably broken, and the parties seek a divorce pursuant to Section 3301(c) of the Divorce Code; or in the alternative, the parties have lived separate and apart for a period of at least two years and the marriage of the parties is irretrievably broken, and the Plaintiff seeks a divorce pursuant to Section 3301(d) of the Divorce Code." For more information about the grounds for divorce, see the section in Chapter 4 on "Grounds for Divorce."

☞ In paragraph 6, if you and your spouse have been involved in any previous divorce or annulment case (between the two of you; this does not refer to prior marriages), fill in the county and case number. If not, type in the word "none" after the word "except."

☞ For paragraph 7, if you and your spouse have a written agreement concerning support, visitation, alimony, and property division; cross out the words "have not." If you do not have a written agreement concerning any of these matters, cross out the word "have." If you have a written agreement about some of these matters, but not others, you will need to ask the court clerk how this paragraph should be completed. For example, if you do have a written agreement on everything except alimony, the words "have not" apply to alimony, but the word "have" applies to everything else.

☞ If there is an agreement as to the division of your property, cross out the heading "Count II - Equitable Distribution," and the four paragraphs under that heading. If there is not an agreement as to the division of your property, in paragraph 9, fill in the dates of your marriage and separation.

☞ If you are not asking for alimony, cross out the heading "Count III - Alimony," and the four paragraphs under that heading.

☞ If you are requesting alimony and you are the husband, cross out the words "her" and "herself" in the parentheses in paragraph 12; if you are the wife cross out the words "him" and "himself."

☞ In paragraph 13 (if you are requesting alimony), if you are the husband cross out the word "herself" in the parentheses; if you are the wife cross out the word "himself."

☞ If there are no minor or dependent children, so that there is no need for child support, cross out the heading "Count IV - Support for Children," and the seven paragraphs under that heading. If you are requesting child support, follow the next five instructions.

☞ In paragraph 15, fill in the number of unemancipated children, and each of the name, age, sex, date of birth, and current address (residence) of each child.

☞ In paragraph 16, fill in the names of all children for whom you are seeking child support.

☞ In paragraph 17, cross out either "is" or "is not," to indicate if you are receiving public assistance for yourself or any of children. If you are receiving assistance, fill in the amount and payment period.

☛ In paragraph 18, fill in your spouse's estimated annual income, and the estimated value of your spouse's assets. Also cross out either "net" or "gross," to indicate which figure you are using.

☛ In paragraph 19, if your spouse has not been contributing support for you or your child cross out the word "or" and the entire sentence afterward. If your spouse has been contributing, cross out the paragraph through the word "or," then fill in the payment information.

☛ If you are not asking for alimony during the divorce process, attorney's fees, or costs and expenses; cross out the heading "Count V - Alimony Pendente Lite, Counsel Fees, Costs and Expenses," and the four paragraphs under that heading. If you are requesting any of these items: in paragraph 22, if you are the husband cross out the word "herself," and if you are the wife cross out the word "himself."

☛ If there are no children (so that there is no need to determine - custody), cross out the heading "Count VI - Custody," and the four paragraphs under that heading. If custody needs to be determined, follow the next five instructions.

☛ In paragraph 24, fill in the addresses where the children have resided during the past five years, and the name and current address of the persons with whom they resided.

☛ In paragraph 25, cross out "has" or "has not," and "child" or "children," to reflect whether there are any other court cases. If you have participated in such a court case, fill in the name of the county where the case was filed, the case number, and a brief statement as to the status or disposition of the case. The *status* refers to a case still in progress.

Example: "Answer filed and hearing set for April 1, 2002," or "case continued until May 15, 2002, based upon Plaintiff's statement that this COMPLAINT IN DIVORCE was about to be filed".

Disposition refers to the end result of a case that has been concluded.

Example: "Petition dismissed," or "judgment entered granting alternate weekend visitation to husband."

☞ In paragraph 26, cross out "has" or "has no," and "child" or "children," to reflect whether you are aware of any other custody case that is currently pending. If there is another custody case, fill in the name of the county where the case was filed, the case number, and a brief explanation of the nature and status of that case.

☞ In paragraph 27, cross out "knows" or "does not know," and "child" or "children," to indicate whether anyone besides you and your spouse claim any custody or visitation rights regarding your children. If someone does claim such rights, fill in a brief explanation.

☞ In the paragraph after paragraph 28, beginning with the word "Wherefore," cross out the words "custody," "partial custody," or "visitation right," to reflect what you want the court to order.

☞ Sign your name on the line after the word "By," and below the signature line, cross out the words "Attorneys for."

☞ In the section titled "Verification to Complaint in Divorce," sign your name on the line marked "Plaintiff," and fill in the date on the line indicated. This takes the place of the AFFIDAVIT in other counties, which is described in the following section. (see form 5, p.181.)

AFFIDAVIT

Except in Philadelphia County, you will also need to complete an AFFIDAVIT (see form 5, p.181), according to the following instructions:

☞ Complete the top portion of the form according to the instructions in Chapter 7 on page 69.

☞ After the words "County Of" type in the name of the county where you will sign your forms before a notary.

☞ *Do not* sign this form yet! After you have completed all of the necessary forms, you will sign them before a notary public.

☞ Staple this AFFIDAVIT (form 5) to the back of your COMPLAINT IN DIVORCE (form 4).

The four forms explained above (CIVIL COVER SHEET, NOTICE TO CLAIM AND DEFEND RIGHTS, COMPLAINT IN DIVORCE, and AFFIDAVIT) will be filed with the prothonotary, and copies of all but the CIVIL COVER SHEET will be delivered to your spouse as described in Chapter 7.

NOTE : *In Philadelphia County, this form is replaced by the verification provision at the end of the COMPLAINT IN DIVORCE. (see form 26, p.209.)*

COUNTY COURT OF COMMON PLEAS INTAKE

Except in Philadelphia County, the COUNTY COURT OF COMMON PLEAS INTAKE is filed to provide the court with basic information. (see form 6, p.182.)

☞ Fill in the date (the case number will be filled in when you file).

☞ Check the appropriate box to describe the type of divorce case that applies to you.

☞ Type in your name and address under the heading for the "Plaintiff/Petitioner."

☞ Type in your spouse's name and address under the heading for the "Defendant/Respondent."

DOMESTIC RELATIONS INCOME AND EXPENSE STATEMENT

Except if you are filing in Philadelphia County, a DOMESTIC RELATIONS INCOME AND EXPENSE STATEMENT should be filled out by you, and one should be filled out by your spouse. (see form 7, p.183.) This form will give the court basic information about your employment, available health insurance, and income. It is fairly clear what information is required.

For income and deduction information, refer to your pay records. Be sure to convert all amounts to whatever your pay interval happens to be.

Example: If you are paid weekly, but union dues are only deducted once a month, you will need to convert the union dues to a weekly amount.

The following forms will not be filed until ninety days have passed since you filed the COMPLAINT IN DIVORCE:

- MARITAL PROPERTY SETTLEMENT AGREEMENT (form 9)

- ACKNOWLEDGEMENT (form 10)

- AFFIDAVIT OF CONSENT (form 16 and form 17)

- WAIVER OF NOTICE OF INTENTION TO REQUEST ENTRY OF DIVORCE DECREE UNDER § 3301 OF THE DIVORCE CODE (form 30)

- SUPPORT GUIDELINE COMPUTATIONS—CHILD SUPPORT (form 8)

- PRAECIPE TO TRANSMIT RECORD (form 12)

- DECREE OF DIVORCE (form 18)

- RECORD OF DIVORCE OR ANNULMENT (form 20)

- NOTICE OF INTENTION TO RETAKE PRIOR NAME (form 24)

MARITAL PROPERTY SETTLEMENT AGREEMENT

Whether you and your spouse agreed upon everything from the start, or went through extensive negotiations to reach an agreement, you need to put your agreement into writing. Even if you do not agree upon everything, you should put what you do agree upon into a written settlement agreement. (Remember, child custody agreements will be handled through the court's custody office, and support agreements will be handled by the support counselor. See Chapter 4 for more information.)

It is common practice for attorneys to create a custom MARITAL PROPERTY SETTLEMENT AGREEMENT for each case. There is not a pre-approved, or standard, MARITAL PROPERTY SETTLEMENT AGREEMENT form (except in Philadelphia County). To help you, we have provided a form in Appendix C. (see form 9, p.185.) Use it as a guide to create your own form, or do some additional research and create a form all your own. In Philadelphia County, you should use form 33 or the form you obtain form the Family Law Clerk (which will be virtually identical to form 33). In any event, you need to specifically and succinctly list, and clearly spell out, how your property and debts will be divided.

To complete the MARITAL PROPERTY SETTLEMENT AGREEMENT (see form 9, p.185):

- ☞ Complete the caption portion of the form according to the instructions in Chapter 7, page 69. Make certain your names appear just as they appear on your original COMPLAINT IN DIVORCE. (see form 4, p.180.)

- ☞ Just below the document title ("Marital Property Settlement Agreement") fill in the date, and the name and address information indicated for you and your spouse. Make sure you choose "Husband" or "Wife" for each party by crossing off the one that does not apply. (i.e. If the plaintiff is the wife, cross off "Husband.")

☛ After the word "Witnesseth," fill in the date you and your spouse were married and the date you filed for divorce where indicated.

☛ List the property that the wife will keep in paragraph 3, and the property the husband will keep in paragraph 4. Describe each item clearly. Refer to the **PROPERTY INVENTORY** (form 1) that you filled out earlier.

NOTE: *These paragraphs provide that each of you will keep your own clothing and personal effects, unless otherwise noted. Therefore, it is not necessary to list all of these items. However, if there are any such items that are particularly valuable (such as a mink coat or valuable jewelry items), it may be a good idea to list them just to make it clear who is to get the item.*

Do not list real estate here, as that will be listed in paragraph 8. Do not list pension, retirement, or profit sharing plans; bank, credit union, or other financial institution accounts; stocks, bonds, and other securities; or IRAs here, as these will all be listed in paragraph 7.

☛ In paragraph 5, list all of the debts for which the wife will be responsible to pay.

☛ In paragraph 6, list all of the debts for which the husband will be responsible to pay. Give the name of the person or company to whom the debt is owed and the account number. Refer to the **DEBT INVENTORY** (form 2) you filled out earlier. Remember that if the debt was incurred by you and your spouse jointly, you are both still liable for repayment. In other words, even if your spouse agrees to pay it, if he or she fails to pay, then the creditor can still come after you. You could then drag your spouse back to court for violating the settlement agreement, but your credit rating would still be damaged.

Example: Joe and Mary have a joint credit card. In their settlement agreement, they agree that Joe can keep the card and will be responsible to pay. If Joe runs up charges over the next year then declares bankruptcy, the credit card company can still sue Mary, and the delinquency will go on Mary's credit report. She can drag Joe back to court, but if he is in such bad financial shape that he had to declare bankruptcy, there is probably very little the court can do to force him to repay her. And there is nothing the court can do to repair her credit rating. What Mary should have done was to be sure the credit card was cancelled, and let Joe get his own credit card after the divorce.

☞ In paragraph 7, list all pension, retirement, or profit sharing plans; bank, credit union, or other financial institution accounts; stocks, bonds, and other securities; or IRAs that you and your spouse own, either separately or jointly. Identify each item clearly.

Example: "ABC Corporation pension plan," "First National Bank checking account, #39288409," "200 shares of XYZ Corporation common stock," etc.

For each item, indicate whether it will be kept by you or your spouse.

☞ In paragraph 8, you will list all of your real estate. (If you do not own any real estate, after the words "Real Estate" type in "No real estate is owned by the parties, either individually or jointly.")

There are several options for dealing with the division of your real estate.

First, one of you may buy-out the other and keep the property. If this is your desire, type in: "Husband and Wife own real estate located at _____{give address of property}. Husband / Wife shall retain the property. Husband/ Wife shall remit the amount of $_____{insert amount agreed upon} to cover buy-out of the other party's interest."

Another option is to sell the property and divide the proceeds. To do this, type in: "Husband and Wife own real estate located at _____*{give address of property}*. The parties agree that the property shall be sold and the proceeds divided (after payment of commissions, closing costs and other sales expenses) as follows: _____*{insert percentage or dollar amount}* to Husband, and _____*{insert percentage or dollar amount}* to Wife."

A third option is simply for one of the parties to get the property (such as where there is more than one piece of real estate or one party will get more of the personal property). To do this, type in: "Husband / Wife shall retain real estate located at _____*{give address of property}.*" If one of you will keep the property and be responsible for an existing mortgage, be sure to list the mortgage as that person's responsibility in paragraph 5 or 6. As with other joint debts, be aware that you will both still be responsible for a joint mortgage debt even if one of you keeps the property and agrees to pay the mortgage.

Example: Martin and Marsha get divorced and agree that Marsha will keep the house and pay the mortgage. Marsha fails to make payments and the mortgage company forecloses. When the mortgage company sells the house, it gets $10,000 less than the mortgage balance. The mortgage company then sues Martin for the $10,000. If your spouse is going to keep property that is mortgaged, you should require him or her to get a new mortgage so that only your spouse is responsible to pay.

☛ Paragraph 9 is to indicate any arrangements you and your spouse have regarding alimony and expenses of the divorce case. As it is, this paragraph provides: "Each of the parties hereto releases the other from subsequent claims for alimony, alimony pendente lite, or spousal support, except as follows:" If neither of you are to pay alimony, simply type in the word "None" below that sentence. If you do have an agreement for alimony, you will need to fill in the details.

Example: "Husband shall pay alimony to Wife in the amount of $200 per month, beginning on March 1, 2000, and continuing on the first day of each month thereafter, until February 1, 2005. No alimony shall be paid after February 1, 2005."

☞ After all of the information is filled in, you and your spouse need to go to a notary public and sign this form before the notary. The notary public will provide witnesses to sign your form.

PHILADELPHIA COUNTY MARITAL SETTLEMENT AGREEMENT FORM

In Philadelphia County, use the MARITAL PROPERTY SETTLEMENT AGREEMENT. (see form 33, p.221.) Again, you may find that you need to use the form available from the Family Law Clerk (which will be virtually identical to form 33), but the following instructions will still assist you in completing the form:

☞ Complete the caption portion of the form according to the instructions in Chapter 7, page 69. Make certain your names appear just as they appear on your original COMPLAINT IN DIVORCE. (see form 26, p.209.)

☞ In paragraph 1, fill in the date your COMPLAINT IN DIVORCE was filed.

☞ On the first line in paragraph 2, fill in your name and address. Below that, cross out either the word "Wife" or "Husband," whichever does not apply to you. On the line below the word "and," fill in your spouse's name and address. Below that, cross out either the word "Wife" or "Husband," whichever does not apply to your spouse. On the next set of lines, fill in the date and place of your marriage.

☞ In paragraph 3, fill in the name, age, and date of birth of each child.

☛ The second page of the form is to explain how you and your spouse will divide your property and debts. In the first paragraph on the second page, cross out either "Wife" or "Husband" in two places (whichever does not apply to you), then list the debts you will be responsible to pay on the lines below.

☛ In the second paragraph on the second page, cross out either "Wife" or "Husband" in two places (whichever does not apply to your spouse), then list the debts your spouse will be responsible to pay on the lines below.

☛ In other sections on the second page you will list the property you will keep and the property your spouse will keep, again crossing out the word "Wife" or "Husband" as appropriate.

☛ The last line on the second page is to fill in the address of your home. Again, in various places you will need to cross out the word "Wife" or "Husband" as appropriate.

☛ On the last page of the form are spaces for you and your spouse to sign and date the form, and for a witness for each of you. You will also need to cross out the word "Wife" or "Husband" in various places as appropriate.

ACKNOWLEDGEMENT

You and your spouse will each need to complete an ACKNOWLEDGEMENT (form 10), and staple them to your MARITAL PROPERTY SETTLEMENT AGREEMENT. (see form 9, p.185 or form 33, p.221.) Therefore, make two copies of the ACKNOWLEDGEMENT. (see form 10, p.189.) These forms should not be filed until after ninety days have passed since you filed your COMPLAINT IN DIVORCE. (see form 4, p.180 or form 26, p.209.)

To complete the ACKNOWLEDGEMENT (see form 10, p.189):

☛ Complete the caption portion of the form according to the instructions in Chapter 7, page 69.

☞ In the first paragraph, fill in the date your COMPLAINT IN DIVORCE (form 4 or form 26) was filed.

☞ In the second paragraph, fill in the name of the county in which you filed your divorce case.

☞ Staple your form 10 and your spouse's form 10 to the back of your MARITAL PROPERTY SETTLEMENT AGREEMENT (form 9 or form 33).

☞ Sign your name before a notary public (your spouse will sign his or her ACKNOWLEDGEMENT form before a notary also).

AFFIDAVIT OF CONSENT AND WAIVER OF NOTICE OF INTENTION TO REQUEST ENTRY OF DIVORCE DECREE

If you and your spouse agree on everything, and you both sign a MARITAL PROPERTY SETTLEMENT AGREEMENT (form 9) and each sign an ACKNOWLEDGMENT (form 10), you still must complete an AFFIDAVIT OF CONSENT (see form 16, p.197) and your spouse must complete an AFFIDAVIT OF CONSENT. (see form 17, p.198.)

NOTE: *If you are filing in Philadelphia County, you and your spouse will instead each file a Waiver of Notice of Intention to Request Entry of a Divorce Decree Under § 3301(c) of the Divorce Code. (see form 31, p.218.)*

AFFIDAVIT OF
CONSENT

To complete the AFFIDAVIT OF CONSENT (form 16 and form 17), you and your spouse need to:

☞ Complete the caption portion of the form according to the instructions in Chapter 7, page 69.

☞ Fill in the date your COMPLAINT IN DIVORCE was filed on the lines in paragraph 1 (month/day/year).

☞ Fill in the date at the bottom of the form, and sign on the signature line. Be sure you sign on form 16 (marked "Plaintiff" below the signature line) and your spouse signs on form 17 (marked "Defendant" below the signature line).

PHILADELPHIA COUNTY WAIVER OF NOTICE FORM

If you are filing in Philadelphia County, you will need to make two copies of the WAIVER OF NOTICE OF INTENTION TO REQUEST ENTRY OF A DIVORCE DECREE UNDER § 3301(C) OF THE DIVORCE CODE, one for you and one for your spouse. (see form 31, p.218.) To complete the WAIVER OF NOTICE OF INTENTION TO REQUEST ENTRY OF A DIVORCE DECREE UNDER § 3301(C) OF THE DIVORCE CODE (see form 31, p.218), you and your spouse need to:

☞ Complete the caption portion of the form according to the instructions in Chapter 7, page 69.

☞ Fill in the date at the bottom of the form.

☞ On your form, sign on the signature line, and cross out the word "Defendant" below the signature line. On your spouse's form, your spouse will sign on the signature line, then cross out the word "Plaintiff" below the signature line.

SUPPORT GUIDELINE COMPUTATIONS— CHILD SUPPORT

The Support Guideline Computations—Child Support is a form that complies with Pennsylvania Supreme Court Rules, and will help you properly compute the child support amount using the guidelines in the Pennsylvania Statutes. (see form 8, p.184.) Fill in this form according to the instructions in the section of Chapter 6 on "Child Support." Be sure to complete all sections of the form. This will help you figure out the child support amount for your marital property settlement agreement.

PRAECIPE TO TRANSMIT RECORD

The PRAECIPE TO TRANSMIT RECORD is the paper the judge will sign (in addition to a DECREE OF DIVORCE) in order to formally grant your divorce. (see form 12, p.191.) If you are filing in Philadelphia County, use form 28 or the form provided by the Clerk.

To complete the PRAECIPE TO TRANSMIT RECORD (see form 12, p.191):

☛ Complete the caption portion according of the form to the instructions in Chapter 7, page 69.

☛ Fill out the vital statistics form, called RECORD OF DIVORCE OR ANNULMENT. (see form 20, p.201.) See page 105 for instructions.

☛ Attach a signed copy of your MARITAL PROPERTY SETTLEMENT AGREEMENT (form 9) with your and your spouse's signed ACKNOWLEDGMENT forms (form 10).

☛ Attach a signed AFFIDAVIT OF CONSENT (form 16) for you, and a signed AFFIDAVIT OF CONSENT (form 17) for your spouse. Both of these forms must be signed within thirty days of filing the final PRAECIPE TO TRANSMIT RECORD documents with the prothonotary.

☛ Attach three blank copies of the DECREE OF DIVORCE (form 18) for the judge to sign and emboss. These will be sent to you after the judge grants your divorce.

PHILADELPHIA COUNTY PRAECIPE TO TRANSMIT RECORD

To complete the Philadelphia County PRAECIPE TO TRANSMIT RECORD (see form 28, p.215):

☛ Complete the caption portion of the form according to the instructions in Chapter 7, page 69.

☛ In paragraph 1, cross out "3301(d)." The mutual consent procedure is under Section 3301(c).

☛ In paragraph 2, type in the date the COMPLAINT IN DIVORCE was served on your spouse, and the manner in which it was served.

(For example: "April 1, 2002, by certified mail, return receipt requested," or "April 1, 2002, by personal service.")

☞ In paragraph 3(a), fill in the date you signed the AFFIDAVIT OF CONSENT, and the date your spouse signed the AFFIDAVIT OF CONSENT, on the appropriate lines. Leave paragraph 3(b) blank, as that subparagraph does not apply to the mutual consent divorce.

☞ In paragraph 4(a), state whether there are any custody or support issues pending before the court.

☞ In paragraph 4(b), state whether there have been custody, support, or other issues removed, discontinued, or no otherwise no longer before the court.

☞ In paragraph 4(c), state if there are any agreements as to custody, child support, spousal support, or property settlements between you and your spouse.

☞ In paragraph 4(d), type in "yes" or "no" to indicate whether you and your spouse have signed a MARITAL PROPERTY SETTLEMENT AGREEMENT. If you answer "yes," you will need to attach a copy of your agreement to the decree form you obtained from the clerk.

☞ In paragraph 5, fill in the date the NOTICE OF INTENT TO FILE PRAECIPE TO TRANSMIT was mailed to the defendant. (see form 29, p.216.)

☞ Sign your name on the signature line, and below the signature line cross out the words "Attorney for" and the word "Defendant."

11. Attach a signed copy of the NOTICE OF INTENT TO FILE PRAECIPE TO TRANSMIT. (see form 29, p.216.)

DECREE OF DIVORCE

You will also need to send the judge a DECREE OF DIVORCE. (see form 18, p.199.) If you are filed in Philadelphia County, you will need to obtain a decree form from the Family Court Clerk. Philadelphia County has two decree forms for divorces using the mutual consent procedure under Section 3301(c) of the Divorce Code: one (titled "Decree") for cases with a Marital Property Settlement Agreement, and one (titled "Decree and Order") for cases without such an agreement. To complete form 18 or the Philadelphia County form, all you need to fill in is the caption information according to the instructions in Chapter 7, page 69. The judge will fill in the rest of the form and sign it.

RECORD OF DIVORCE OR ANNULMENT

The RECORD OF DIVORCE OR ANNULMENT (see form 20, p.201), which is more commonly called the "vital statistics form," must be filled out once the divorce is granted. This form will be forwarded by the prothonotary's office to the Vital Records office of the Pennsylvania Department of Health. The form clearly indicates what information is to be filled in for each block. If you have any questions, the prothonotary can help you fill in the blanks. The following information may also be of some help:

- ☞ In item 17A, fill in the total number of children you and your spouse have, regardless of whether they are now adults or minors.

- ☞ In item 17B, fill in the number of children under the age of 18.

- ☞ In item 21, fill in "irretrievable breakdown."

- ☞ Items 23 and 24 will be filled in by the prothonotary.

If you filed in Philadelphia County, you may need to obtain this form from the Family Court Clerk. It is identical to form 20, but Philadelphia is very particular about using their forms.

NOTICE OF INTENTION TO RETAKE PRIOR NAME

If you are the wife, and you desire to resume your maiden name, or another name you had before you were married, you will need to file a NOTICE OF INTENTION TO RETAKE PRIOR NAME. (see form 24, p.205.) This form may be filed along with the PRAECIPE TO TRANSMIT RECORD, and should be filed no later than five days after the entry of your DIVORCE DECREE.

To complete the NOTICE OF INTENTION TO RETAKE PRIOR NAME (form 24):

- ☞ Complete the caption portion according to the instructions in Chapter 7, page 69.

- ☞ In the main paragraph, cross out either "Plaintiff" or "Defendant," whichever does not apply to you, fill in the date of your Divorce Decree, and fill in the prior name you wish to resume.

- ☞ Leave the "Signature" line blank, because you will need to sign before a notary public.

- ☞ On the line below the words "To Be Known As," type in the prior name you will resume.

- ☞ Take this form to a notary public and sign your current name (not the prior name you are resuming) on the "Signature" line. The notary will fill in the lower part of this form.

STANDARD UNCONTESTED DIVORCE 9

The standard uncontested divorce procedure will be used in one of the following situations:

1. Your spouse cannot be located.

2. Your spouse is not willing to cooperate in the mutual consent procedure, but does not actively oppose the divorce.

In this procedure, your legal basis for divorce will be that you and your spouse have lived separate and apart for a period of at least two years, and your marriage is irretrievably broken. This means you are filing under Section 3301(d) of the Divorce Code. (Your COMPLAINT IN DIVORCE will still also refer to Section 3301(c), just in case you manage to reach an agreement at some point.)

FORMS

To begin your divorce case, you will file many of the same forms as you would for the mutual consent procedure described in Chapter 8. Therefore, you will need to refer to Chapter 8 for instructions on completing these forms. Any differences in how you will complete the forms will be mentioned below. See Chapter 7 for instructions on filing the forms with the prothonotary and delivering them to your spouse.

The following forms will be completed and filed with the prothonotary's office in order to begin your case (except in Philadelphia County, which is discussed below):

☐ CIVIL COVER SHEET (form 13). Follow the instructions for this form in Chapter 8.

☐ NOTICE TO DEFEND AND CLAIM RIGHTS (form 3).

☐ COMPLAINT IN DIVORCE (form 4).

☐ AFFIDAVIT (form 5), stapled to your COMPLAINT IN DIVORCE.

☐ COURT OF COMMON PLEAS INTAKE (form 6).

☐ DOMESTIC RELATIONS INCOME AND EXPENSE STATEMENT (form 7).

The following forms will be filed later to conclude your case:

☐ SUPPORT GUIDELINE COMPUTATIONS—CHILD SUPPORT (form 8), if you and your spouse have any minor children.

☐ NOTICE OF INTENTION TO REQUEST ENTRY OF DIVORCE DECREE (form 21)

☐ PRAECIPE TO TRANSMIT RECORD (form 12). In this procedure you will not have a MARITAL PROPERTY SETTLEMENT AGREEMENT (form 9), ACKNOWLEDGMENT (form 10), or AFFIDAVIT OF CONSENT (form 16 and form 17) to attach (unless you and your spouse reach an agreement during the course of the procedure).

☐ NOTICE TO FILE SOCIAL SECURITY NUMBERS (form 23).

☐ DECREE OF DIVORCE (form 18).

☐ RECORD OF DIVORCE OR ANNULMENT (form 20).

☐ NOTICE OF INTENTION TO RETAKE PRIOR NAME (form 24), if you are the wife and desire to resume using a former name.

If you and your spouse are able to reach an agreement at some point before the final hearing, you will need to use the following forms:

☐ MARITAL PROPERTY SETTLEMENT AGREEMENT (form 9).

☐ ACKNOWLEDGMENT (form 10) signed by you, and stapled to your MARITAL PROPERTY SETTLEMENT AGREEMENT.

☐ ACKNOWLEDGMENT (form 10) signed by your spouse, and stapled to your MARITAL PROPERTY SETTLEMENT AGREEMENT.

☐ AFFIDAVIT OF CONSENT (form 16), signed by you.

☐ AFFIDAVIT OF CONSENT (form 17), signed by your spouse.

To help you keep track of your case, the preceding list of forms is reproduced as Checklist 3 in Appendix B.

PHILADELPHIA FORMS

As we have mentioned before, Philadelphia County has its own forms. Although forms 25 through 36 in Appendix C are recreated from the Philadelphia County forms, you may still need to obtain these forms from the Family Court Clerk. Even if you are able to use the forms in Appendix C, you will still need to obtain the Decree forms from the Family Court Clerk.

If you are filing in Philadelphia County, you will file these forms to begin your case:

☐ DOMESTIC RELATIONS INFORMATION SHEET (form 25)

☐ COMPLAINT IN DIVORCE (form 26).

Follow the instructions for this form in Chapter 8, with the following exceptions:

☞ In paragraph 7, you will just cross out the word "have" because you will not have a property settlement agreement at the time you file your COMPLAINT IN DIVORCE.

☞ In the paragraph after paragraph 7, beginning with the word "Wherefore," you will not add any additional words because you will not have any agreement to attach.

☐ PLAINTIFF'S AFFIDAVIT UNDER SECTION 3301(D) OF THE DIVORCE CODE (form 27).

NOTE: *A copy of this form, along with a blank copy of the DOMESTIC RELATIONS INFORMATION SHEET (form 25) must be sent to your spouse.*

To complete your case in Philadelphia County, you will file these forms:

☐ NOTICE OF INTENTION TO REQUEST ENTRY OF § 3301(D) DIVORCE DECREE (CASES UNDER SECTION 3301(C) OF THE DIVORCE CODE) (form 35) [if your spouse is **not** represented by an attorney]; or NOTICE OF INTENTION TO REQUEST ENTRY OF DIVORCE (form 34) [if your spouse **is** represented by an attorney]

☐ PRAECIPE TO TRANSMIT RECORD (form 28).

Follow the instructions for this form in Chapter 8, with the following exceptions:

☞ In paragraph 1, cross out "3301(c);" **do not** cross out "3301(d)."

☞ Leave paragraph 3(a) blank. Instead, you will fill in paragraph 3(b). In paragraph 3(b)(1), fill in the date you signed the PLAINTIFF'S AFFIDAVIT UNDER SECTION 3301(D) OF THE DIVORCE CODE. (see form 27, p.214.) In paragraph 3(b)(2), fill in the date you filed the PLAINTIFF'S AFFIDAVIT. In paragraph 3(b)(3), fill in the date the PLAINTIFF'S AFFIDAVIT was served on your spouse.

☞ In this procedure you will not have a MARITAL PROPERTY SETTLEMENT AGREEMENT (form 33), therefore, type in "No" in paragraph 4(d).

☐ Decree. You will need to obtain the appropriate decree form from the Family Court Clerk. There are two decree forms for use in a divorce under Section 3301(d); one (titled "Decree") for cases without a MARITAL PROPERTY SETTLEMENT AGREEMENT, and one (titled "Decree and Order") for cases with a MARITAL PROPERTY SETTLEMENT AGREEMENT.

☐ RECORD OF DIVORCE OR ANNULMENT (form 20), commonly called the "vital statistics form."

☐ NOTICE OF INTENTION TO RETAKE PRIOR NAME (form 24), if you are the wife and desire to resume using a former name.

If you and your spouse are able to reach an agreement at some point before the final hearing, you will need to use the following forms:

☐ MARITAL PROPERTY SETTLEMENT AGREEMENT (form 33)

☐ ACKNOWLEDGMENT (form 10, or a similar form if you are required to use a form obtained from the clerk) signed by you, and stapled to your MARITAL PROPERTY SETTLEMENT AGREEMENT.

☐ ACKNOWLEDGMENT (form 10, or a similar form if you are required to use a form obtained from the clerk) signed by your spouse, and stapled to your MARITAL PROPERTY SETTLEMENT AGREEMENT.

☐ WAIVER OF NOTICE OF INTENTION TO REQUEST ENTRY OF A DIVORCE DECREE UNDER § 3301(C) OF THE DIVORCE CODE (form 30), signed by the plaintiff (you).

☐ WAIVER OF NOTICE OF INTENTION TO REQUEST ENTRY OF A DIVORCE DECREE UNDER § 3301(C) OF THE DIVORCE CODE (form 30), signed by the defendant (your spouse).

To help you keep track of your case, the preceding list of forms is reproduced as Checklist 4 in Appendix B.

PROCEDURES

Basically, the procedure is as follows:

1. You complete and file the necessary forms.

2. You have your spouse served with copies of the necessary forms.

3. You file other appropriate forms with the prothonotary in order to complete the case.

Once you have prepared your initial papers, you will need to have copies of your NOTICE TO DEFEND AND CLAIM RIGHTS (see form 3, p.179), COMPLAINT IN DIVORCE (see form 4, p.180), and AFFIDAVIT (see form 5, p.181) delivered to your spouse. Refer to Chapter 7 for information about how to have these paper delivered. If you cannot find your spouse, see the subsection below entitled "If You Cannot Find Your Spouse."

NOTE: *In Philadelphia County you will just have the* **COMPLAINT IN DIVORCE** *(form 26) delivered, as this form includes a Notice of Defend and Claim Rights and a verification section instead of the Affidavit.*

YOUR SPOUSE'S RESPONSE

After receiving copies of the divorce papers, your spouse may contact an attorney. The attorney will then notify you that he or she is representing your spouse. Typically, there is no immediate time-frame regarding a response from your spouse. If your spouse responds, he or she will file a written response with the prothonotary, or contact you by mail, telephone, in person, or through his or her attorney. However, (in less frequent cases) your spouse may choose to ignore the divorce papers. If this occurs, you should proceed through the spousal support hearing (and, if children are involved, the child support/custody hearing) channels. This process will usually rouse your spouse out of unresponsiveness and compel him or her to take action.

IF YOU CANNOT FIND YOUR SPOUSE

If your spouse has disappeared, and you are unable to locate him or her, you should serve your divorce papers on him or her by sending them Certified Mail/Return Receipt Requested to your spouse's last known address.

You may also wish to publicize your filing with an ad in the legal section of your local newspaper. This will substantiate your attempt to locate your spouse. There is also the chance that either your spouse will see the ad or someone he or she knows will see the ad, which will prompt him or her to contact you so you can proceed with your divorce quickly.

SUPPORT AND CUSTODY HEARINGS

Regardless of whether your spouse responds, you should proceed with the spousal support and child support/custody hearings. Keep in mind that the spousal support order and child custody/support order may be put into effect even if your spouse does not appear. Hearings will take place in your spouse's absence if it is determined that proper notice has been given to your spouse. If such orders are entered and not honored by your spouse, you may ask the court to hold your spouse in contempt.

Contested Divorce 10

Unfortunately, most divorces are neither simple nor uncomplicated. Should you find yourself in a contested divorce, additional forms are required that will facilitate the initiation and processing of your matter. This chapter will outline forms required in a contested divorce and explain how they must be completed.

Forms

To begin your contested divorce case, you will file many of the same forms as the mutual consent procedure and the standard divorce procedure. You may have begun your case hoping a settlement could be reached, but are now in a contested situation. Refer to Chapter 8 for instructions on completing these forms. Any differences in completing these forms will be mentioned below. See Chapter 7 for instructions about filing the forms and delivering them to your spouse.

The following forms will be completed and filed with the prothonotary's office in order to begin your case:

- ☐ CIVIL COVER SHEET (form 13). Follow the instructions for this form in Chapter 8;

- ☐ NOTICE TO DEFEND AND CLAIM RIGHTS (form 3);

☐ COMPLAINT IN DIVORCE (form 4);

NOTE: *You should be able to use the grounds as stated in paragraph 7 of the* COMPLAINT IN DIVORCE *form (1) if your spouse also wants a divorce, but is arguing about one or more of the other issues (i.e., property division, child custody, child support, or alimony); or (2) if your spouse does not want the divorce and you are willing to wait for the required two year period of living separate and apart.*

If your spouse will not agree to the divorce, you have not met the two year separation requirement, and you do not want to wait, you will need to add one or more of the fault grounds (and be able to prove it). If you believe you need to use fault grounds, you should consult an attorney.

☐ AFFIDAVIT (form 5), stapled to your COMPLAINT IN DIVORCE;

☐ COURT OF COMMON PLEAS INTAKE (form 6); and,

☐ DOMESTIC RELATIONS INCOME AND EXPENSE STATEMENT (form 7).

The following forms will be filed later:

☐ SUPPORT GUIDELINE COMPUTATIONS - CHILD SUPPORT (form 8), if you and your spouse have any minor children;

☐ NOTICE OF INTENTION TO REQUEST ENTRY OF DIVORCE DECREE (form 21) and COUNTERAFFIDAVIT UNDER § 3301(D) OF THE DIVORCE CODE (form 22). Both of these forms must be filed after your spouse is served with the COMPLAINT IN DIVORCE, and before submission of the final documents necessary to conclude the divorce. Both of these forms must be served on your spouse and filed with the Office of the Prothonotary;

☐ PRAECIPE TO TRANSMIT RECORD (form 12). In this procedure you will not have a MARITAL PROPERTY SETTLEMENT AGREEMENT (form 9), ACKNOWLEDGMENT (form 10), or AFFIDAVIT OF CONSENT (forms 16 and 17) to attach (unless you and your spouse reach an agreement during sometime during the process);

☐ NOTICE TO FILE SOCIAL SECURITY NUMBERS (form 23);

☐ DECREE OF DIVORCE (form 18);

☐ RECORD OF DIVORCE OR ANNULMENT (form 20); and,

☐ NOTICE OF INTENTION TO RETAKE FORMER NAME (form 24), if you are the wife and desire to resume using a former name.

If you and your spouse are able to reach an agreement at some point before the final hearing, you will need to use the following forms:

☐ MARITAL PROPERTY SETTLEMENT AGREEMENT (form 9);

☐ ACKNOWLEDGMENT (form 10) signed by you, and stapled to your MARITAL PROPERTY SETTLEMENT AGREEMENT;

☐ ACKNOWLEDGMENT (form 10) signed by your spouse, and stapled to your MARITAL PROPERTY SETTLEMENT AGREEMENT;

☐ AFFIDAVIT OF CONSENT (form 16), signed by you; and,

☐ AFFIDAVIT OF CONSENT (form 17), signed by your spouse.

To help you keep track of your case, the preceding list of forms is reproduced as Checklist 5 in Appendix B.

PHILADELPHIA COUNTY FORMS

If you are filing in Philadelphia County, you will file these forms to begin your case:

☐ DOMESTIC RELATIONS INFORMATION SHEET (form 25);

☐ COMPLAINT IN DIVORCE (form 26). Follow the instructions for this form in Chapter 8, with the following exceptions:

☞ In paragraph 5 you will type: "The parties have lived separate and apart for a period of at least two years and the marriage of the parties is irretrievably broken, and the Plaintiff seeks a divorce pursuant to Section 3301(d) of the Divorce Code; or in the alternative, pursuant to Section 3301(c) of the Divorce Code."

☞ In paragraph 7, you will just cross out the word "have" because you will not have a property settlement agreement at the time you file your COMPLAINT IN DIVORCE.

☞ In the paragraph after paragraph 7, beginning with the word "Wherefore," you will not add any additional words because you will not have any agreement to attach.

☐ PLAINTIFF'S AFFIDAVIT (form 27).

NOTE: *A copy of this form, along with a blank copy of the* DOMESTIC RELATIONS INFORMATION SHEET *(form 25) must be sent to your spouse.*

To complete your case in Philadelphia County, you will file these forms:

☐ NOTICE OF INTENTION TO REQUEST ENTRY OF §3301(D) DIVORCE DECREE (CASES UNDER SECTION 3301(C) OF THE DIVORCE CODE) (form 35) [if your spouse is *not* represented by an attorney]; or NOTICE OF INTENTION TO REQUEST ENTRY OF DIVORCE (form 34) [if your spouse *is* represented by an attorney];

☐ PRAECIPE TO TRANSMIT RECORD (form 28). Follow the instructions for this form in Chapter 8, with the following exceptions:

☞ In paragraph 1, cross out "3301(c);" *do not* cross out "3301(d)."

☞ Leave paragraph 3(a) blank. Instead, you will fill in paragraph 3(b). In paragraph 3(b)(1), fill in the date you signed the PLAINTIFF'S AFFIDAVIT (form 27). In paragraph 3(b)(2), fill in the date you filed the PLAINTIFF'S AFFIDAVIT (form 27). In paragraph 3(b)(3), fill in the date the PLAINTIFF'S AFFIDAVIT (form 27) was served on your spouse.

☞ In this procedure you will not have a MARITAL PROPERTY SETTLEMENT AGREEMENT (form 33), therefore, type in "No" in paragraph 4(d).

☐ Decree. You will need to obtain the appropriate decree form from the Family Court Clerk. There are two decree forms for use in a divorce under Section 3301(d); one (titled "Decree") for cases without a MARITAL PROPERTY SETTLEMENT AGREEMENT, and one (titled "Decree and Order") for cases with a MARITAL PROPERTY SETTLEMENT AGREEMENT;

❏ **RECORD OF DIVORCE OR ANNULMENT** (form 20), commonly called the "vital statistics form;" and,

❏ **NOTICE OF INTENTION TO RETAKE PRIOR NAME** (form 24), if you are the wife and desire to resume using a former name.

If you and your spouse are able to reach an agreement at some point before the final hearing, you will need to use the following forms:

❏ **MARITAL PROPERTY SETTLEMENT AGREEMENT** (form 33);

❏ **ACKNOWLEDGMENT** (form 10, or a similar form if you are required to use a form obtained from the clerk) signed by you, and stapled to your **MARITAL PROPERTY SETTLEMENT AGREEMENT**;

❏ **ACKNOWLEDGMENT** (form 10, or a similar form if you are required to use a form obtained from the clerk) signed by your spouse, and stapled to your **MARITAL PROPERTY SETTLEMENT AGREEMENT**;

❏ **WAIVER OF NOTICE OF INTENTION TO REQUEST ENTRY OF A DIVORCE DECREE UNDER § 3301(D) OF THE DIVORCE CODE** (form 30), signed by the plaintiff (you); and,

❏ **WAIVER OF NOTICE OF INTENTION TO REQUEST ENTRY OF A DIVORCE DECREE UNDER § 3301(C) OF THE DIVORCE CODE** (form 30), signed by the defendant (your spouse).

To help you keep track of your case, the preceding list of forms is reproduced as Checklist 6 in Appendix B.

PROCEDURES

This book cannot transform you into a trial lawyer. It can be very risky to attempt to handle a contested case yourself, although it has been done. There are several differences between a contested and an uncontested case.

First, in an uncontested case the judge will usually go along with whatever you and your spouse have worked out. In a contested case you need to prove that you are entitled to what you are asking for. This means you will likely have one or more court hearings before a master or judge, where you will need to present papers and testimony as evidence. You may need to have witnesses testify for you.

Second, you may have to do some extra work to get the evidence you need, such as by sending out subpoenas, or even hiring a private investigator. Also, you will need to pay extra attention to assure that your spouse is properly notified of any court hearings, and that he or she is sent copies of any papers you file with the prothonotary office.

When it becomes apparent that you have a contested divorce, it is probably time to consider hiring an attorney, especially if the issue of child custody is involved. If you are truly ready to go to war over custody, it shows that this is an extremely important matter for you, and you may want to get professional assistance. You can predict a contested case when your spouse is seriously threatening to fight you every inch of the way, or when he or she hires an attorney.

On the other hand, you should not assume that you need an attorney just because your spouse has hired one. Sometimes it will be easier to deal with the attorney than with your spouse. The attorney is not as emotionally involved and may see your settlement proposal as reasonable. So discuss issues with your spouse's attorney first to see if matters can be worked out. You can always hire your own lawyer if your spouse's lawyer is not reasonable. Please be very cautious about signing any papers until you are certain you understand exactly what they mean. You may want to have an attorney review any papers prepared by your spouse's lawyer before you sign them.

Basically, the procedure in a contested case is as follows:

1. You complete and file the necessary forms.
2. You have your spouse served with copies of the necessary forms.
3. Your spouse files a response indicating that he or she is contesting one or more issues.

4. You and your spouse attend one or more hearings, and present evidence in order to get the disputes resolved.

5. You file other appropriate forms with the prothonotary in order to complete the case.

NOTIFYING YOUR SPOUSE

Once you have prepared your initial papers, you will need to have copies of your NOTICE TO DEFEND AND CLAIM RIGHTS (see form 3, p.179), COMPLAINT IN DIVORCE (see form 4, p.180), and AFFIDAVIT (see form 5, p.181) delivered to your spouse. Refer to Chapter 7 for information about how to have these paper delivered. If you cannot find your spouse, see the discussion below.

NOTE: *In Philadelphia County you will just have the COMPLAINT IN DIVORCE (form 26) delivered, as this form includes a NOTICE OF DEFEND AND CLAIM RIGHTS and a verification section instead of the Affidavit.*

YOUR SPOUSE'S RESPONSE

After receiving copies of the divorce papers, your spouse may contact an attorney. The attorney will then notify you that he or she is representing your spouse. Typically, there is no immediate time-frame regarding a response from your spouse. If your spouse responds, he or she will file a written response with the prothonotary, or contact you by mail or telephone, in person, or through his or her attorney.

If your spouse also wants a divorce, but is arguing about one or more of the other issues (i.e., property division, child custody, child support, or alimony), you may still proceed with the divorce on the grounds of the marriage being irretrievably broken. However, if your spouse does not want the divorce, the only way you can proceed is on the grounds of the marriage being irretrievably broken and you and your spouse having lived separate and apart for at least two years (or by using one of the fault grounds as mentioned on pages 33, 34, and 35; which is beyond the scope of this book).

If you already meet the two year requirement, you may proceed with the divorce. If you do not meet the two year requirement, you will need to file a new Complaint in Divorce after the two year requirement is met.

Aside from deciding if you want a lawyer, there are two main procedural differences between an uncontested and the contested divorce. First, you will need to be more prepared for the hearing. Second, you will not be able to file your consent and consent waiver documents since it is likely that your spouse will not sign them.

THE HEARING   The next chapter will discuss how to prepare for the issues to be argued at certain hearings. Under Pennsylvania law, a spouse refusing to consent to a divorce may delay the process for up to two years.

THE MASTER'S HEARING 11

A *family law master* may be appointed by the court to hear testimony on some or all of the issues in your divorce case, with the exception of custody and paternity claims. A *master's hearing* is generally unnecessary in no-fault divorce cases where no defense is raised or where the parties consent. Referral to a master is within the discretion of the judge. Either party may file a motion to request a referral to a master, or the judge may make the referral on his or her own.

A family law master is a court officer, who has the responsibility of seeing that your case proceeds in a fair and equitable manner. The master must see that the relevant issues of your case are thoroughly explored, but the master is not responsible for helping either you or your spouse present your cases. The master is responsible for notifying the parties (or their attorneys) of all hearings, and for preparing a *Report and Recommendation* regarding the issues he or she is called upon to resolve.

You will be required to compensate the master. The amount of compensation will be determined by the judge. The amount must be fair, taking into consideration the time involved and the ability of the parties to pay. You may also be required to pay for a court reporter to take down the testimony and prepare a transcript of the hearing.

In resolving issues regarding the fair and equitable division of the marital assets and debts, the master will consider the various factors listed in the Divorce Code, as discussed in Chapter 5. When alimony is at issue, the Report and Recommendation must include findings of fact showing the reasons, according to the factors set forth in the Divorce Code, that alimony is or is not necessary. If alimony is recommended, the Report and Recommendation must also state the nature, amount, duration, and manner of payment. A similar analysis will be conducted on any claim for child support or counsel fees and expenses.

In an uncontested case, the master is required to file the record, a transcript of the testimony, and his or her Report and Recommendation, within twenty days after the hearing. In a contested case, this must be done within thirty days after the transcript is received from the court reporter. The master must also notify both parties when the Report and Recommendation is filed.

Although the master's Report and Recommendation is entitled to significant weight, it is not binding on the judge. If you disagree with the findings contained in the Report and Recommendation, you must file exceptions in order to preserve the issues for appeal. It is strongly suggested that you do not attempt to represent yourself in an appeal from a master's hearing. The issues in such an appeal will become extremely complicated, and require the skilled legal assessment of an attorney.

PREPARATION

You will need to contact the master (or the master's secretary or clerk) to schedule a hearing. See Chapter 7 for more information about setting a hearing date.

NOTIFYING YOUR SPOUSE

You will need to notify your spouse of when the hearing will be. Even if you can call your spouse on the phone, you are required to send a formal NOTICE OF HEARING. (see form 19, p.200.) Fill in the NOTICE OF HEARING according to the instructions in Chapter 7. Then make three copies of the NOTICE OF HEARING. Mail one copy to your spouse, file the original with the prothonotary, and keep two copies for yourself.

WHAT PAPERS
TO BRING

What papers to bring. Bring your copies of:

- all documents filed in your case, these should also be in the prothonotary's file;

- your most recent paystub, Federal income tax return, and W-2 forms, and any other papers showing your or your spouse's financial situation;

- any papers showing your or your spouse's income, expenses, property, and debts; and,

- the MARITAL PROPERTY SETTLEMENT AGREEMENT (form 9 or form 33) if you have any issues upon which agreement has been reached.

THE HEARING

Your hearing will probably not take place in a large courtroom like you see on TV or in the movies. It will most likely be in what looks more like a conference room. Generally, the master will be at the head of a table, with you and your spouse on either side. The master may start the hearing by summarizing what you are there for. The master will ask you and your spouse if you have any additional evidence to present, and then ask each of you any questions he or she may have. The master will review the papers you filed with the prothonotary, and will probably ask you whether you understand and agree with what is in the papers.

GROUNDS FOR
DIVORCE

The master will also ask you to explain why your marriage is "irretrievably broken." Just tell the master why you are getting divorced.

Example 1: "We just do not have any interests in common anymore, and have drifted apart."

Example 2: "My husband has had several affairs."

FINANCIAL
INFORMATION

You will then give a copy of whatever papers you have to show the financial situation (such as current paystub showing an increase in pay, or a current bank statement showing a new balance). The master may ask to see any papers you have to prove what you have put in your DOMESTIC RELATIONS INCOME AND EXPENSE STATEMENT (see form 7, p.183) that you filed at the support office. If child support or alimony is to be paid, you will also need to show the master your support and alimony information and copies of the support orders you obtained from the support office. The master will review all documents submitted.

If you and your spouse have signed a MARITAL PROPERTY SETTLEMENT AGREEMENT (see form 9, p.185 or form 33, p.221), present it to the master if it has not already been filed with the prothonotary. If you and your spouse have reached any other agreements, tell the master.

Your basic job at the hearing is to answer the master's questions and give him or her the information needed to give you a divorce.

PROPERTY DIVISION

If there are any items that you and your spouse have not yet agreed upon, tell the master what these items are. Refer to Chapter 10, relating to the contested divorce, for more information about how to handle these unresolved issues. Be prepared to make a suggestion as to how these matters should be settled, and to explain to the master why your suggestion is the best solution. If the master asks for any information that you have not brought with you, tell the master that you do not have it with you but you will be happy to provide the information by the end of the following day. Just be sure you get the papers to him or her.

At the hearing, the master will probably try to get you to work out your disagreements, but he or she will not put up with arguing for very long. In the end the master will divide the items you cannot agree upon, or may order you to sell those items and divide the money you get equally.

On the few items that are really important to you, it may be necessary for you to try to prove why you should get them. It will help if you can convince the master of one or more of the following:

- you paid for the item out of your own earnings or funds;

- you are the one who primarily uses that item;

- you use the item in your employment, business, or hobby;

- you are willing to give up something else you really want in exchange for that item (of course you will try to give up something from your "do not care" or your "like to have" list); or,

- the item is needed for your children (assuming you will be awarded custody).

The best thing you can do is make up a list of how you think the property should be divided. Make it a reasonably fair and equal list, regardless of how angry you are at your spouse. Even if the master changes some of it to appear fair to your spouse, you will most likely get more of what you want than if you do not offer a suggestion.

NOTE: *This is not an exception to the negotiating rule of letting your spouse make the first offer, because at this point you are no longer just negotiating with your spouse. You are now negotiating with the master. You are trying to impress the master with your fairness—not trying to convince your spouse.*

Special problems arise if a claim of nonmarital property becomes an issue. This may be in terms of your spouse trying to get your nonmarital property, or in terms of you trying to get property you feel your spouse in wrongly claiming to be nonmarital. Basically, nonmarital property is property either of you had before you were married and kept separate.

It is also a good idea to have any papers that prove that the property you claim to be nonmarital property is actually nonmarital property. These would be papers showing that:

- you bought the item before you were married (such as dated sales receipts);

- you inherited the item as your own property (such as certified copies of wills and probate court papers); and,

- you got the property by exchanging it for property you had before you got married, or for property you received as a gift or through an inheritance (such as a statement from the person you made the exchange with, or a receipt showing what was exchanged).

If you want to get at assets your spouse is claiming are nonmarital assets, you will need to collect the following types of evidence:

- papers showing that you helped pay for the asset (such as a check that you wrote, or bank statements showing that your money went into the same account that was used to make payments on the asset);

    Example: Suppose your spouse purchased a house before you got married. During your marriage you made some of the mortgage payments with your own checking account (you will have cancelled checks, hopefully with the mortgage account number on them, to prove this). At other times, you deposited some of your paychecks into your spouse's checking account, and your spouse wrote checks from that account to pay the mortgage (again, there should be some bank records and cancelled checks that show that this was done). Since you contributed to the purchase of the house, you can claim some of the value of the house as a marital asset.

- papers showing that you paid for repairs of the asset. If you paid for repairs on the home, or a car your spouse had before you were married, you can claim part of the value; and,

- papers showing that the asset was improved, or increased in value during your marriage.

    Example 1: Your spouse owned the house before you were married. During your marriage you and your spouse added a family room to the house. This will enable you to make a claim for some of the value of the house.

Example 2: Your spouse owned the house before you were married. The day before you got married, the house was worth $85,000. Now the house is appraised at $115,000. You can claim part of the $30,000 of increased value.

CONCLUDING THE HEARING

At the end of the hearing, if you have prepared a proposed DECREE OF DIVORCE (form 18 or the decree form that may be required in your county), tell the master ("I have a proposed Decree of Divorce"), and hand him or her the original. You should have two extra copies of the DECREE OF DIVORCE with you, one for yourself and one for your spouse. You should also bring two envelopes, one addressed to yourself, and one addressed to your spouse, and two stamps. This is in case the master wants to review the DECREE OF DIVORCE and mail it to you later, instead of signing it at the hearing.

If the master wants you to make any changes in the DECREE OF DIVORCE, make a careful note of exactly what the master wants (ask him or her to explain it again if you did not understand the first time), then tell the master that you will make the correction and deliver corrected copies. Of course if the changes are minimal, then you may be able to change the DECREE OF DIVORCE right at the hearing and have the master sign it.

When the hearing is over, thank the master and leave.

If any serious problems develop at the hearing (such as your spouse's attorney starts making a lot of technical objections, or the master gives you a hard time), just tell the master you would like to continue the hearing so you can retain an attorney and then go get one.

You will also need to fill out the RECORD OF DIVORCE OR ANNULMENT (see form 20, p.201), which is commonly called the "vital statistics form." See Chapter 8 for more information on this form.

SPECIAL CIRCUMSTANCES 12

Every divorce is as different and unique as an individual's fingerprint. Many unusual circumstances arise and each person's divorce case presents a variety of situations that must be addressed. Chapter 12 will outline some key special circumstances, which occur most frequently in divorce matters.

WHEN YOU CANNOT AFFORD COURT COSTS

If you cannot afford to pay court costs, such as filing fees and sheriff service fees, you should go to the prothonotary office, which is usually located at your county courthouse. Tell the prothonotary that you wish to file for divorce, but are unable to afford the filing fee and other court costs. The prothonotary will verify your financial status to determine if you qualify, and provide you with the necessary information and forms to have the court costs either waived or reduced.

If you are involved in a custody case and are experiencing financial hardship, your local legal aid office will often appoint an attorney (at no charge to you) to handle your custody case. These are volunteer lawyers who offer their time and service to handle such cases.

PROTECTING YOURSELF, YOUR CHILDREN, AND YOUR PROPERTY

Some people have three special concerns when getting prepared to file for a divorce: 1. fear of physical attack by their spouse; 2. fear that their spouse will try to take the marital property and hide it; and, 3. fear that their spouse will take the children and leave the court's jurisdiction. There are additional legal papers you can file if you feel you are in either of these situations.

PROTECTING YOURSELF

If you are fearful of physical attack, you should regard your fears with great seriousness. Domestic violence is the use of physical, emotional, or sexual abuse to control another in a close relationship. *Physical abuse,* or battering, is a pattern of physical assaults, threats, or restraints. *Emotional abuse* is a manipulation of feelings by making the partner feel worthless, helpless, or afraid. *Sexual abuse* is mistreatment by means of sexual demands or insults. Remember that nothing that you (as the victim) have done justifies a violent reaction. Marriage does not give one person the right to abuse the other.

If you are abused, please be aware that help awaits you. Call the police if you require immediate care, help, or protection. Seek medical attention for any injuries, and make certain that all injuries are documented. Go to the house of a relative, neighbor, or friend if your home is unsafe. Call the shelter service organization in your area—day or night—for confidential assistance (you can get the phone number from the police).

If you are in a violent situation, your shelter service organization will provide you with legal counsel and set up the appropriate court hearings to put a Protection From Abuse (PFA) Order into effect. PFA orders are legally binding court orders that serve to legally preclude your spouse from further endangering you or your children. You should carefully consider the options that are available to you. Remember that there *are* alternatives to living in a violent relationship.

Some important facts to consider: One-third of all children who witness battering of their mother develop behavioral and emotional problems. Children are emotionally scarred by witnessing family violence. Many of these children grow up to repeat the pattern, either as a victim or as an abuser. Violence usually becomes more frequent and more serious over time, unless the victim takes action to break the cycle. Women who report attacks are less likely to be repeatedly attacked. Partners in abusive situations can be of any race, religion, social or economic group, age, or educational background.

Battering is the single greatest cause of injury to women—more than rapes, muggings, and auto accidents combined. Four million American women are battered each year, and every fifteen seconds a woman in the United States is beaten by her husband, ex-husband, or boyfriend. At the time of this writing, it is estimated that four thousand women die each year because of domestic violence. Do not let yourself become a statistic.

PROTECTING YOUR CHILDREN

If you are worried that your spouse may try to kidnap your children, you should make sure that the day care center, babysitter, relative, or whomever you leave the children with at any time, is aware that you are in the process of a divorce and that the children are only to be released to you personally (not to your spouse or to any other relative, friend, etc.). To prevent your spouse from taking the children out of the United States, you can apply for a passport for each child. Once a passport is issued, the government will not issue another. So get their passport and lock it up in a safe deposit box. (This will not prevent them from being taken to Canada or Mexico, where passports are not required, but will prevent them from being taken overseas.)

You can also file a motion to prevent the removal of the children from the state and to deny passport services. Also, the State Department usually requires both parents to sign a passport application for a minor. If only one parent applies, they are required to show proof of legal custody. You should be able to obtain forms for this motion from the prothonotary or your local law library.

PROTECTING YOUR PROPERTY

If you genuinely fear that your spouse will try to remove money from bank accounts and try to hide important papers showing what property you own, you may want to take this same action before your spouse can. However, you can make a great deal of trouble for yourself with the judge if you do this to try to get these assets for yourself. So, make a complete list of any property you do take, and be sure to include these items in your lists of property. You may need to convince the judge that you only took these items temporarily, in order to preserve them until a hearing was set.

Also, do not spend any cash you take from a bank account, or sell or give away any items of property you take. Any cash should be placed in a separate bank account, without your spouse's name on it, and kept separate from any other cash you have. Any papers, such as deeds, car titles, stock or bond certificates, etc., should be placed in a safe deposit box, without your spouse's name on it. The idea is not to take these things for yourself, but to get them in a safe place so your spouse can not hide them and deny they ever existed.

If your spouse is determined and resourceful, there is no guaranteed way to prevent the concerns discussed in this chapter from happening. All you can do is put as many obstacles in his or her way as possible, and prepare for him or her to suffer legal consequences (e.g., fine or jail) for acting improperly.

TEMPORARY SUPPORT AND CUSTODY

TEMPORARY SUPPORT

If your spouse has left you with the children, the mortgage and monthly bills, and is not helping you financially, you may want to ask the court to order the payment of support for you and the children during the divorce procedure. Of course, if you were the only person bringing in income and have been paying all the bills, do not expect to get any temporary support. To request temporary support, go to the support office in your county. The personnel at the support office will assist you in seeking temporary support.

TEMPORARY
CUSTODY

To seek a temporary child custody order, you will need to go to the support or custody office for your county and request a hearing for support or custody. To complete the PETITION FOR TEMPORARY CUSTODY (see form 14, p.193):

- ☞ Complete the top portion of the form according to the instructions in Chapter 7, page 69.

- ☞ Type your name on the line in the first, unnumbered paragraph.

- ☞ In paragraph 1, type your name on the first line, and your street address, city, and zip code on the other lines.

- ☞ In paragraph 2, type in your spouse's name and address on the appropriate lines.

- ☞ In paragraph 3, fill in the date you were married, and the date you and your spouse separated.

- ☞ In paragraph 4, fill in the date of birth for each child.

- ☞ In paragraph 5, indicate who your children are currently living with. Type in the word "Petitioner" if the children are in your physical custody, or the "Respondent" if they are in the physical custody of your spouse. If the children are living with someone other than you or your spouse (such as a grandparent, aunt, or friend) fill in the name of the person they are living with, and that person's relationship to you.

- ☞ In paragraph 6, list any medical conditions of any of the children. If there are no special significant medical conditions, type in "none."

- ☞ In paragraph 7, indicate the number of years during which the children have resided with you. List the addresses at which the children have resided, indicating whether they resided with their mother, father, or both.

- ☞ In paragraph 8, state the full name of the biological mother of the child or children.

- ☞ In paragraph 9, state the full name of the biological father of the child or children.

- ☞ In paragraph 13, circle the parent listed that indicates with whom you are requesting the children take residence.

- ☞ After the section that begins with the word "Wherefore," you will need to circle one of the words in item 2. Circle the word "mother" or "father" (whichever applies to you). If the child has been removed from Pennsylvania, also circle the word "Pennsylvania."

- ☞ Sign your name on the line marked "Name."

- ☞ Complete the Verification page, which is the last page of the form: Complete the top portion according to the instructions in Chapter 7, page 196. Then type in your name on the line in the main paragraph, and date and sign the form on the lines indicated.

If you have a good reason for not notifying your spouse in advance, this form needs to be presented to the judge, along with the ORDER OF COURT. (see form 15, p.196.) To complete the ORDER OF COURT (form 15):

- ☞ Complete the top portion according to the instructions at the beginning of Chapter 7, page 69.

- ☞ On the second line of the main paragraph, after the word "Plaintiff," type in your name.

- ☞ On the third line, type in the number of children.

- ☞ On the fourth line, type in the name or names of the children. The judge will fill in the other blank spaces.

Call the secretary for the judge or master, and say that you would like to submit a "motion for temporary custody," and ask how you should do this. The secretary may tell you to come in with your papers at a certain time, to mail them, or to submit them to the prothonotary's office. Just follow the instructions.

If possible, you should notify your spouse of your motion just before you go see the judge or master, either verbally or by mailing, and file a CERTIFICATE OF SERVICE. (see form 11, p.190.) Otherwise, be prepared to tell the judge or master why you were unable to notify your spouse. To complete the ORDER OF COURT (see form 15, p.196), all you need to do is complete the top portion of the form. The judge or master will either fill in the rest, or tell you how to fill in the rest.

Once you have a signed copy of the ORDER OF COURT (form 15), mail or deliver a copy to your spouse. Then complete a CERTIFICATE OF SERVICE (form 11) to show that you have notified your spouse. If your spouse has not filed any papers with the court yet, you should have the ORDER OF COURT served on him or her by the sheriff (refer back to Chapter 7 for information on having papers served by the sheriff). It is important to be able to satisfy the judge that your spouse knew about the ORDER OF COURT if you need to collect support arrearages, or file contempt proceedings for violation of the custody order.

TAXES

As you are no doubt aware, the United States' income tax code is complicated and ever-changing. For this reason, it is impossible to give detailed legal advice with respect to taxes in a book such as this. Any such information could easily be out of date by the time of publication. Therefore, it is strongly recommended that you consult your accountant, lawyer, or whomever prepares your tax return, about the tax consequences of a divorce. A few general concerns are discussed in this chapter, to give you an idea of some of the tax questions that can arise.

PROPERTY AND TAXES

You and your spouse may be exchanging title to property as a result of your divorce. Generally, there will not be any tax to pay as the result of such a transfer. However, whomever gets a piece of property will be responsible to pay any tax that may become due upon sale.

The Internal Revenue Service (IRS) has issued numerous rulings about how property is to be treated in a divorce. You need to be very careful if you are transferring any tax shelters, or other complicated financial arrangements. Be sure to read the following section on "Alimony and Taxes" because fancy property settlements are asking for tax problems.

ALIMONY AND TAXES

Alimony can cause the most tax problems of any aspect of divorce. The IRS is always making new rulings on whether an agreement is really alimony, or is really property division. The basic rule is that *alimony* is treated as income to the person receiving it, and as a deduction for the person paying it. Therefore, in order to manipulate the tax consequences, many couples try to show something as part of the property settlement, instead of as alimony, or the reverse. As the IRS becomes aware of these "tax games," it issues rulings on how it will view a certain arrangement. If you are simply talking about the regular, periodic payment of cash, the IRS will probably not question that it is alimony. But if you try to call it a property settlement, you may run into problems. The important thing is to consult a tax expert if you are considering any unusual or creative property settlement or alimony arrangements.

CHILD SUPPORT AND TAXES

There are simple tax rules regarding child support:

- whomever has custody gets to claim the children on his or her tax return (unless both parents file a special IRS form agreeing to a different arrangement each year);

- child support is not considered income to the parent receiving it; and,

- the parent paying child support cannot deduct it.

If you are sharing physical custody, the parent with whom the child lives for the most time during the year is entitled to claim the child. The IRS form to reverse this must be filed each year. If you and your spouse agreed that you can claim the child (although you do not have custody), get your spouse to sign an open-ended form that you can file each year, so that you do not have to worry about it each year. A phone call to the IRS can help you get answers to questions on this point.

PENSION PLANS

Pension plans, or retirement plans, of you and your spouse are marital assets. They may be very valuable assets. If you and your spouse are young, and have not been working very long, you may not have pension plans worth worrying about. Also, if you have both worked, and have similar pension plans, it may be best just to include a provision in your settlement agreement that "each party shall keep his or her own pension plan." But if you have been married a long time, and your spouse worked while you stayed home to raise the children, your spouse's pension plan may be worth a lot of money, and may be necessary to see you through retirement.

If you and your spouse cannot agree on how to divide a pension plan, you should see an attorney. The valuation of pension plans, and how they are to be divided, is a complicated matter that you should not attempt.

MILITARY

If your spouse is member of the armed services or any branch of the United States military, it is strongly suggested that you retain an attorney to represent you. Military divorces are quite complicated and interject a completely foreign element into the divorce process, which this book does not explore.

CONCLUSION

Divorce will always be a traumatic and difficult process in one's life. Understanding the system and legal entanglements associated with a divorce can make the process less painful. We hope that this book serves you well in maneuvering through the maze of legal issues and facilitates the result that you desire.

GLOSSARY

A

abandon.   To intentionally and permanently give up, surrender, leave, desert or relinquish all interest or ownership in property, a home or other premises, a right of way, and even a spouse, family, or children. To abandon children can mean to have no contact and give no support for a year or more.

accept.   To receive something with approval and intention to keep it. This use often arises on the question of accepting a payment which is late or not complete or accepting the "service" (delivery) of legal papers.

acceptance.   Receiving something from another with the intent to keep it, and/or showing that this was based on a previous agreement.

acceptance of service.   Agreement by a defendant (or his/her attorney) in a legal action to accept a complaint or other petition (like divorce papers) without having the sheriff or process server show up at the door. The agreement of "acceptance of service" must be in writing or there is no proof that it happened. In most jurisdictions there is a form entitled "receipt and acknowledgment of acceptance of service" or similar language which must be signed, dated and sent back to the attorney who sent the complaint or petition.

accrue.   Growing or adding to, such as interest on a debt or investment which continues to accumulate.

acknowledgment.   The section at the end of a document where a notary public verifies that the signer of the document states he/she actually signed it.

action.   A lawsuit in which one party (or parties) sues another.

admit.   To state something is true in answering a complaint filed in a lawsuit. The defendant will admit or deny each allegation in his or her answer filed with the court.

adopt.   To take on the relationship of parent to child of another person, particularly (but not necessarily) a minor, by official legal action.

adoption.   The taking of a child into one's family, creating a parent to child relationship, and giving him or her all the rights and privileges of one's own child, including the right to inherit as if the child were the adopter's natural child.

adultery.   Consensual sexual relations when one of the participants is legally married to another. In some states it is still a crime and in many states it is grounds for divorce for the spouse of the married adulterer. The criminal charges are almost never brought, and in those states in which there is no-fault divorce (or dissolution), adultery is legally not relevant. Until the 1970s, in community property states adultery was grounds for giving the person cheated upon most of the couple's property, often resulting in lurid and long trials and grist for scandal newspapers.

affidavit.   Any written document in which the signer swears under oath before a notary public or someone authorized to take oaths (like a County Clerk), that the statements in the document are true.

agreement.   Any meeting of the minds, even without legal obligation and/or in law, another name for a contract including all the elements of a legal contract: offer, acceptance, and consideration (payment or performance), based on specific terms.

alimony.   Support paid by one ex-spouse to the other as ordered by a court in a divorce (dissolution) case. Alimony is also called "spousal support" in California and some other states. Usually it is paid by the male to his ex, but in some cases a wealthy woman may have to pay her husband.

allegation.   Statement of claimed fact contained in a complaint (a written pleading filed to begin a lawsuit), a criminal charge, or an affirmative defense (part of the written answer to a complaint). Until each statement is proved it is only an allegation.

allege.   To claim a fact is true, commonly in a complaint which is filed to commence a lawsuit, in an "affirmative defense" to a complaint, in a criminal charge of the commission of a crime or any claim.

amend.   To alter or change by adding, subtracting, or substituting.

antenuptial (prenuptial) agreement.   A written contract between two people who are about to marry, setting out the terms of possession of assets, treatment of future earnings, control of the property of each, and potential division if the marriage is later dissolved.

appeal.   To ask a higher court to reverse the decision of a trial court after final judgment or other legal ruling.

appraiser.   A professional who makes appraisals of the value of property. Some specialize in real property, and others in other types of assets from rugs to rings.

appreciation.   The increase in value through the natural course of events as distinguished from improvements or additions.

arrears.   Money not paid when due, usually the sum of a series of unpaid amounts, such as rent, installments on an account or promissory note, or monthly child support. Sometimes these are called "arrearages."

asset.   Generally any item of property that has monetary value, including articles with only sentimental value (particularly in the estates of the dead). Assets are shown in balance sheets of businesses and inventories of probate estates.

B

bifurcate. The order or ruling of a judge that one issue in a case can be tried to a conclusion or a judgment given on one phase of the case without trying all aspects of the matter. A typical example is when the judge will grant a divorce judgment without hearing evidence or making a ruling on such issues as division of marital property, child custody or spousal support (alimony). Thus the parties can be free of each other promptly while still fighting over other issues at their leisure. In a negligence case when the question of responsibility (liability) is clearly in doubt or rests on some legal technicality, the court may bifurcate the issues and hear evidence on the defendant's liability and decide that issue before going ahead with a trial on the amount of damages. If the court rules there is no liability, then the amount of damages is meaningless and further trial is necessary.

bifurcation. The act of a judge in dividing issues before a trial so that one issue will be ruled upon before hearing evidence on the other issue. *See also* **bifurcate.**

breach of contract. Failing to perform any term of a contract, written or oral, without a legitimate legal excuse. This may include not completing a job, not paying in full or on time, failure to deliver all the goods, substituting inferior or significantly different goods, not providing a bond when required, being late without excuse, or any act which shows the party will not complete the work.

C

capital gains. The difference between the sales price and the original cost (plus improvements) of property. Capital gains taxes can be a terrible financial shock to individuals who bought a house or business many years ago for the going price and now find it is highly valued, greatly due to inflation.

case law. Reported decisions of appeals courts and other courts which make new interpretations of the law and, therefore, can be cited as precedents. These interpretations are distinguished from "statutory law," which is the statutes and codes (laws) enacted by legislative bodies; "regulatory law," which is regulations required by agencies based on statutes; and in some states, the common law, which is the generally accepted law carried down from England.

child.   A person's natural offspring, or, generally a person 14 years and under. A "child" should be distinguished from a "minor" who is anyone under 18 in almost all states.

child custody.   A court's determination of which parent, relative or other adult should have physical and/or legal control and responsibility for a minor (child) under 18. Child custody can be decided by a local court in a divorce or if a child, relative, close friend or state agency questions whether one or both parents is unfit, absent, dead, in prison or dangerous to the child's well-being. In such cases custody can be awarded to a grandparent or other relative, a foster parent or an orphanage or other organization or institution. While a divorce is pending the court may grant temporary custody to one of the parents, require conferences or investigation (in some states, if the parents cannot agree, custody is automatically referred to a mediator, commissioner or social worker) before making a final ruling. There is a difference between physical custody, which designates where the child will actually live, and legal custody, which gives the custodial person(s) the right to make decisions for the child's welfare. If the parents agree, the court can award joint custody, physical and/or legal. Joint legal custody is becoming increasingly common.

child support.   Court-ordered funds to be paid by one parent to the custodial parent of a minor child after divorce (dissolution) or separation.

civil procedure.   The complex and often confusing body of rules and regulations set out in both state (usually Code of Civil Procedure) and federal (Federal Code of Procedure) laws which establish the format under which civil lawsuits are filed, pursued and tried.

claim. To make a demand for money, for property, or for enforcement of a right provided by law.

common-law marriage. An agreement between a man and woman to live together as husband and wife without any legal formalities, followed and/or preceded by cohabitation on a regular basis (usually for seven years). Common-law marriage is legal in Alabama, Colorado, Georgia, Idaho, Iowa, Kansas, Montana, Ohio, Oklahoma, Pennsylvania, Rhode Island, South Carolina, Texas and Utah, thereby recognizing a marriage for purposes of giving the other party the rights of a spouse, including inheritance or employee benefits.

complaint. The first document filed with the court (actually with the County Clerk or Clerk of the Court) by a person or entity claiming legal rights against another. The party filing the complaint is usually called the plaintiff and the party against whom the complaint is filed is called the defendant or defendants. Complaints are pleadings and must be drafted carefully (usually by an attorney) to properly state the factual as well as legal basis for the claim.

compromise. An agreement between opposing parties to settle a dispute or reach a settlement in which each gives some ground, rather than continue the dispute or go to trial.

conjugal rights. A spouse's so-called "rights" to the comforts and companionship from his/her mate, meaning sexual relations. Some states allow prisoners to have "conjugal visits" so that they may have private visits and sexual relations with their spouse (or "significant other") in a special room or apartment.

consent. A voluntary agreement to another's proposition or to voluntarily agree to an act or proposal of another.

consent decree. An order of a judge based upon an agreement, almost always put in writing, between the parties to a lawsuit instead of continuing the case through trial or hearing.

contempt of court.   There are essentially two types of contempt: a) being rude, disrespectful to the judge or other attorneys or causing a disturbance in the courtroom, particularly after being warned by the judge; b) willful failure to obey an order of the court. This latter can include failure to pay child support or alimony. The court's power to punish for contempt (called "citing" one for contempt) includes fines and/or jail time (called "imposing sanctions"). Incarceration is generally just a threat and if imposed, usually brief.

contingent fee.   Fee to a lawyer which will be due and payable only if there is a successful conclusion of the legal work, usually winning or settling a lawsuit in favor of the client (particularly in negligence cases), or collecting funds due with or without filing a lawsuit. In many states, such agreements must be in writing and signed by attorney and client. The fee is generally a percentage of the recovery (money won), but may be partly a fee for time worked and partly a percentage. Although fees are negotiable, a standard contingent fee in accident cases is one-third of the money won, unless particular difficulties exist with the case, making the attorney believe he/she has the right to ask for more.

continuance.   Postponement of a date of a trial, hearing or other court appearance to a later fixed date by order of the court, or upon a stipulation (legal agreement) by the attorneys and approved by the court or (where local rules permit) by the clerk of the court.

counselor.   A licensed attorney or lawyer.

court.   The judge, as in "The court rules in favor of the plaintiff", or any official tribunal (court) presided over by a judge or judges in which legal issues and claims are heard and determined. In the United States there are essentially two systems: federal courts and state courts. The basic federal court system has jurisdiction over cases involving federal statutes, constitutional questions, actions between citizens of different states, and certain other types of cases. Its trial courts are District Courts in one or more districts per state, over which there are District Courts of Appeal (usually three-judge panels) to hear appeals from judgments of the

District Courts within the "circuit." There are 10 geographic circuits throughout the nation. Appeals on constitutional questions and other significant cases are heard by the Supreme Court, but only if that court agrees to hear the case. There are also special federal courts such as bankruptcy and tax courts with appeals directed to the District Courts.

court calendar.   List of matters to be heard or set for trial or hearing by a court.

court costs.   Fees for expenses that the courts pass on to attorneys, who then pass them on to their clients or to the losing party. Court costs usually include: filing fees, charges for serving summons and subpoenas, court reporter charges for depositions, court transcripts, and copying papers and exhibits.

court docket.   *See* **docket**.

credibility.   Whether testimony is worthy of belief, based on competence of the witness and likelihood that it is true. Unless the testimony is contrary to other known facts or is extremely unlikely based on human experience, the test of credibility is purely subjective.

cross-examination.   Opportunity for the attorney (or an unrepresented party) to ask questions in court of a witness who has testified in a trial on behalf of the opposing party. The questions on cross-examination are limited to the subjects covered in the direct examination of the witness, but importantly, the attorney may ask leading questions, in which he/she is allowed to suggest answers or put words in the witness' mouth. (For example, "Isn't it true that you told Mrs. Jones she had done nothing wrong?" which is leading, as compared to "Did you say anything to Mrs. Jones?") A strong cross-examination (often called just "cross" by lawyers and judges) can force contradictions, expressions of doubts or even complete obliteration of a witness' prior carefully rehearsed testimony.

custody.   1) holding property under one's control; 2) law enforcement officials' act of holding an accused or convicted person in criminal proceedings, beginning with the arrest of that person; or, 3) in domestic relations (divorce, dissolution) a court's determination of which parent (or other appropriate party) should have physical and/or legal control and responsibility for a minor child.

D

decree.   In general, synonymous with judgment. However, in some areas of the law, the term decree is either more common or preferred as in probates of estates, domestic relations (divorce), admiralty law and in equity (court rulings ordering or prohibiting certain acts).

default judgment.   If a defendant in a lawsuit fails to respond to a complaint in the time set by law (commonly 20 or 30 days), then the plaintiff (suer) can request that the default (failure) be entered into the court record by the clerk, which gives the plaintiff the right to get a default judgment.

defendant.   Party sued in a civil lawsuit or the party charged with a crime in a criminal prosecution. In some types of cases (such as divorce) a defendant may be called a respondent.

direct examination.   First questioning of a witness during a trial or deposition (testimony out of court), as distinguished from cross-examination by opposing attorneys and redirect examination when the witness is again questioned by the original attorney.

dissolution.   Modern, gentler sounding, term for divorce, officially used in California since 1970 and symbolic of the no-fault, non-confrontational approach to dissolving a marriage.

distribution.   Act of dividing up the assets of an estate or trust, or paying out profits or assets of a corporation or business according to the ownership percentages.

docket.   Cases on a court calendar.

domestic relations.   Polite term for the legal field of divorce, dissolution, annulment, child custody, child support and alimony.

domestic violence. Continuing crime and problem of the physical beating of a wife, girlfriend, and/or children, usually by the woman's male partner (although it can also be female violence against a male).

domicile. Place where a person has his/her permanent principal home to which he/she returns or intends to return. This becomes significant in determining in what state a probate of a dead person's estate is filed, what state can assess income or inheritance taxes, where a party can begin divorce proceedings, or whether there is "diversity of citizenship" between two parties which may give federal courts jurisdiction over a lawsuit. Where a person has several "residences" it may be a matter of proof as to which is the state of domicile. A business has its domicile in the state where its headquarters is located.

divorce. Termination of a marriage by legal action, requiring a petition or complaint for divorce.

E

equitable. Just, based on fairness, and not upon legal technicalities.

exhibit. Document or object (including a photograph) introduced as evidence during a trial.

expert testimony. Opinions stated during trial or deposition (testimony under oath before trial) by a specialist qualified as an expert on a subject relevant to a lawsuit or a criminal case. *See also* **expert witness.**

expert witness. Person who is a specialist in a subject, often technical, who may present his/her expert opinion without having been a witness to any occurrence relating to the lawsuit or criminal case. It is an exception to the rule against giving an opinion in trial, provided that the expert is qualified by evidence of his/her expertise, training and special knowledge. If the expertise is challenged, the attorney for the party calling the "expert" must make a showing of the necessary background through questions in court, and the trial judge has discretion to qualify the witness or rule he/she is not an expert, or is an expert on limited subjects. *See also* **expert testimony.**

F

fact. Actual thing or happening, which must be proved at trial by presentation of evidence and which is evaluated by the finder of fact (a jury in a jury trial, or by the judge if he/she sits without a jury).

family. Husband, wife, and children, or all blood relations also, all who live in the same household unit.

H

hearing. Any proceeding before a judge or other magistrate without a jury in which evidence and/or argument is presented to determine some issue of fact or both issues of fact and law. While technically a trial with a judge sitting without a jury fits the definition, a hearing usually refers to brief sessions involving a specific question at some time prior to the trial itself, or such specialized proceedings as administrative hearings.

hearsay. Second-hand evidence in which the witness is not telling what he/she knows personally, but what others have said to him/her and a common objection made by the opposing lawyer to testimony when it appears the witness has violated the hearsay rule. *See also* **hearsay rule.**

hearsay rule. Basic rule that testimony or documents which quote persons not in court are not admissible. Because the person who supposedly knew the facts is not in court to state his/her exact words, the trier of fact cannot judge the demeanor and credibility of the alleged first-hand witness, and the other party's lawyer cannot cross-examine (ask questions of) him or her. However, as significant as the hearsay rule itself are the exceptions to the rule which allow hearsay testimony such as: a) a statement by the opposing party in the lawsuit which is inconsistent with what he/she has said in court.

I

income. Money, goods, or other economic benefit received.

J

joint custody.   In divorce actions, a decision by the court (often upon agreement of the parents) that the parents will share custody of a child.

joint.   Referring to property, rights or obligations which are united, undivided and shared by two or more persons or entities.

jurisdiction.   Authority given by law to a court to try cases and rule on legal matters within a particular geographic area and/or over certain types of legal cases.

L

legal separation.   Court-decreed right to live apart, with the rights and obligations of divorced persons, but without divorce. The parties are still married and cannot remarry. A spouse may petition for a legal separation usually on the same basis as for a divorce, and include requests for child custody, alimony, child support and division of property. For people who want to avoid the supposed stigma of divorce, who hold strong religious objections to divorce or who hope to save a marriage, legal separation is an apparent solution.

legal services.   Work performed by a lawyer for a client.

M

marriage.   Joining of a male and female in matrimony by a person qualified by law to perform the ceremony (a minister, priest, judge, justice of the peace or some similar official), after having obtained a valid marriage license (which requires a blood test for venereal disease in about a third of the states and a waiting period from one to five days in several). The standard age for marriage without parental consent is 18 except for Georgia and Wyoming where it is 16, Rhode Island where women can marry at 16, and Mississippi in which it is 17 for boys and 15 for girls. More than half the states allow marriages at lesser ages with parental consent, going as low as 14 for both sexes in Alabama, Texas, and Utah. Marriages in which the age requirements are not met can be annulled. Fourteen states recognize so-called "common law marriages" which establish a legal marriage for people who have lived together by agreement as husband and wife for a lengthy period of time without legal formalities.

matter of record. Anything, including testimony, evidence, rulings and sometimes arguments, which has been recorded by the court reporter or court clerk. It is an expression often heard in trials and legal arguments that "such and such is a matter of record" as distinguished from actions outside the court or discussions not written down or taped.

mortgage. Document in which the owner pledges his/her/its title to real property to a lender as security for a loan described in a promissory note.

N

negotiation. Transfer of a check, promissory note, bill of exchange or other negotiable instrument to another for money, goods, services or other benefit, or the give-and-take discussion or conference in an attempt to reach an agreement or settle a dispute.

no fault divorce. Divorces (dissolutions) in which neither spouse is required to prove "fault" or marital misconduct on the part of the other.

notary public. Person authorized by the state in which the person resides to administer oaths (swearings to truth of a statement), take acknowledgments, certify documents and to take depositions if the notary is also a court reporter.

O

objection. Lawyer's protest about the legal propriety of a question which has been asked of a witness by the opposing attorney, with the purpose of making the trial judge decide if the question can be asked.

offer. Specific proposal to enter into an agreement with another. An offer is essential to the formation of an enforceable contract. An offer and acceptance of the offer creates the contract.

order.   Direction or mandate of a judge or a court which is not a judgment or legal opinion (although both may include an order) directing that something be done or that there is prohibition against some act. This can range from an order that a case will be tried on a certain date, to an order that a convicted defendant be executed at the state prison.

order to show cause.   Judge's written mandate that a party appear in court on a certain date and give reasons, legal and/or factual, (show cause) why a particular order should not be made.

P

parent.   Lawful and natural father or mother of a person. The word does not mean grandparent or ancestor, but can include an adoptive parent as a replacement for a natural parent.

parental neglect.   Crime consisting of acts or omissions of a parent (including a stepparent, adoptive parent or someone who, in practical terms, serves in a parent's role) which endangers the health and life of a child or fails to take steps necessary to the proper raising of a child. The neglect can include leaving a child alone when he or she needs protection; failure to provide food, clothing, medical attention or education to a child; or placing the child in dangerous or harmful circumstances, including exposing the child to a violent, abusive or sexually predatory person.

pendente lite (pen-den-tay lee-tay).   Latin term for awaiting the litigation (lawsuit). It is applied to court orders (such as temporary child support) which are in effect until the case is tried, or rights which cannot be enforced until the lawsuit is over.

personal property.   *See* **personalty**.

personalty.   Movable assets (things, including animals) which are not real property, money or investments.

plaintiff.   Party who initiates a lawsuit by filing a complaint with the clerk of the court against the defendant(s) demanding damages, performance and/or court determination of rights.

pleading.   1) every legal document filed in a lawsuit, petition, motion and/or hearing, including complaint, petition, answer, demurrer, motion, declaration and memorandum of points and authorities (written argument citing precedents and statutes). Laypersons should be aware that, except possibly for petitions from prisoners, pleadings are required by state or federal statutes and/or court rules to be of a particular form and format: typed, signed, dated, with the name of the court, title and number of the case, name, address and telephone number of the attorney or person acting for himself/herself (in pro per) included. 2) the act of preparing and presenting legal documents and arguments.

praecipe.   A written legal document that commands a person to do something or prove why he or she should not.

R

real property.   Land, structures, firmly attached and integrated equipment (such as light fixtures or a well pump), anything growing on the land, and all "interests" in the property, which may include the right to future ownership (remainder), right to occupy for a period of time (tenancy or life estate), the right to drill for oil, the right to get the property back (a reversion) if it is no longer used for its current purpose (such as use for a hospital, school or city hall), use of airspace (condominium) or an easement across another's property.

relevant.   Having some reasonable connection with, and in regard to evidence in trial, having some value or tendency to prove a matter of fact significant to the case.

residence.   Place where one makes his/her home. However, a person may have his/her state of "domicile" elsewhere for tax or other purposes, especially if the residence is for convenience or not of long standing.

S

separate property.   State laws vary, but generally separate property is, has been, or can be controlled by the spouse owning it.

separation.   Married persons living apart, either informally by one leaving the home or agreeing to "separate" while sharing a residence without sexual relations, or formally by obtaining a "legal separation" or negotiating a "separation agreement" setting out the terms of separate living.

separation agreement.   Agreement between two married people who have agreed to live apart for an unspecified period of time, perhaps forever. The agreement generally covers any alimony (money paid for spousal support), child support, custody arrangements if there are children, payment of bills and management of separate bank accounts.

special master.   Person appointed by the court to carry out an order of the court, such as selling property or mediating child custody cases.

spousal support.   Payment for support of an ex-spouse (or a spouse while a divorce is pending) ordered by the court.

statute.   Federal or state written law enacted by the Congress or state legislature, respectively. Local statutes or laws are usually called "ordinances." Regulations, rulings, opinions, executive orders and proclamations are not statutes.

T

tenancy by the entirety.   Joint ownership of title by husband and wife, in which both have the right to the entire property, and, upon the death of one, the other has title (right of survivorship).

title.   Ownership of real property or personal property, which stands against the right of anyone else to claim the property. In real property, title is evidenced by a deed, judgment of distribution from an estate or other appropriate document recorded in the public records of the county. Title to personal property is generally shown by possession, particularly when no proof or strong evidence exists showing that the property belongs to another or that it has been stolen or known to be lost by another. In the case of automobiles and other vehicles, title is registered with the state's Department of Motor Vehicles, which issues a title document ("pink slip") to the owner.

W

waiver.   Intentional and voluntary giving up of something, such as a right, either by an express statement or by conduct (such as not enforcing a right). A waiver of a legal right in court must be expressed on the record.

witness.   Person who testifies under oath in a trial (or a deposition which may be used in a trial if the witness is not available) with first-hand or expert evidence useful in a lawsuit. A party to the lawsuit (plaintiff or defendant) may be a witness. 2) n. a person who sees an event. 3) n. a person who observes the signing of a document like a will or a contract and signs as a witness on the document attesting that the document was signed in the presence of the witness. 4) v. to sign a document verifying that he/she observed the execution of the document such as a will.

Y

your honor.   Proper way to address a judge in court.

APPENDIX A
PENNSYLVANIA STATUTES

This appendix contains selected portions of Title 23 of the Pennsylvania Consolidated Statutes. It is suggested that you go to your nearest library or law library and review all of Title 23, as well as the Pennsylvania Rules of Court.

PENNSYLVANIA CONSOLIDATED STATUTES

CHAPTER 31

§ 3103.   Definitions

The following words and phrases when used in this part shall have the meanings given to them in this section unless the context clearly indicates otherwise:

"Alimony." An order for support granted by this Commonwealth or any other state to a spouse or former spouse in conjunction with a decree granting a divorce or annulment.

"Alimony pendente lite." An order for temporary support granted to a spouse during the pendency of a divorce or annulment proceeding.

"Divorce." Divorce from the bonds of matrimony.

"Grounds for divorce." The grounds enumerated in section 3301 (relating to grounds for divorce).

"Irretrievable breakdown." Estrangement due to marital difficulties with no reasonable prospect of reconciliation.

"Qualified professionals." Includes marriage counselors, psychologists, psychiatrists, social workers, ministers, rabbis or other persons who, by virtue of their training and experience, are able to provide counseling.

"Separate and apart." Complete cessation of any and all cohabitation, whether living in the same residence or not.

CHAPTER 33

§ 3301.   Grounds for divorce

(a)   **Fault.**—The court may grant a divorce to the innocent and injured spouse whenever it is judged that the other spouse has:

(1) Committed willful and malicious desertion, and absence from the habitation of the injured and innocent spouse, without a reasonable cause, for the period of one or more years.

(2) Committed adultery.

(3) By cruel and barbarous treatment, endangered the life or health of the injured and innocent spouse.

(4) Knowingly entered into a bigamous marriage while a former marriage is still subsisting.

(5) Been sentenced to imprisonment for a term of two or more years upon conviction of having committed a crime.

(6) Offered such indignities to the innocent and injured spouse as to render that spouse's condition intolerable and life burdensome.

(b) Institutionalization.—The court may grant a divorce from a spouse upon the ground that insanity or serious mental disorder has resulted in confinement in a mental institution for at least 18 months immediately before the commencement of an action under this part and where there is no reasonable prospect that the spouse will be discharged from inpatient care during the 18 months subsequent to the commencement of the action. A presumption that no prospect of discharge exists shall be established by a certificate of the superintendent of the institution to that effect and which includes a supporting statement of a treating physician.

(c) Mutual consent.—The court may grant a divorce where it is alleged that the marriage is irretrievably broken and 90 days have elapsed from the date of commencement of an action under this part and an affidavit has been filed by each of the parties evidencing that each of the parties consents to the divorce.

(d) Irretrievable breakdown.—

(1) The court may grant a divorce where a complaint has been filed alleging that the marriage is irretrievably broken and an affidavit has been filed alleging that the parties have lived separate and apart for a period of at least two years and that the marriage is irretrievably broken and the defendant either:

(i) Does not deny the allegations set forth in the affidavit.

(ii) Denies one or more of the allegations set forth in the affidavit but, after notice and hearing, the court determines that the parties have lived separate and apart for a period of at least two years and that the marriage is irretrievably broken.

(2) If a hearing has been held pursuant to paragraph (1)(ii) and the court determines that there is a reasonable prospect of reconciliation, then the court shall continue the matter for a period not less than 90 days nor more than 120 days unless the parties agree to a period in excess of 120 days. During this period, the court shall require counseling as provided in section 3302 (relating to counseling). If the parties have not reconciled at the expiration of the time period and one party states under oath that the marriage is irretrievably broken, the court shall determine whether the marriage is irretrievably broken. If the court determines that the marriage is irretrievably broken, the court shall grant the divorce. Otherwise, the court shall deny the divorce.

(e) No hearing required in certain cases.—If grounds for divorce alleged in the complaint or counterclaim are established under subsection (c) or (d), the court shall grant a divorce without requiring a hearing on any other grounds.

§ 3302. Counseling

(subsection (a) omitted)

(b) Mutual consent.—Whenever mutual consent under section 3301(c) is the ground for divorce, the court shall require up to a maximum of three counseling sessions within the 90 days following the commencement of the action where either of the parties requests it.

(c) Irretrievable breakdown.—Whenever the court orders a continuation period as provided for irretrievable breakdown in section 3301(d)(2), the court shall require up to a maximum of three counseling sessions within the time period where either of the parties requests it or may require such counselling where the parties have at least one child under 16 years of age.

CHAPTER 35

PROPERTY RIGHTS

§ 3501. Definitions

(a) **General rule.**—As used in this chapter, "marital property" means all property acquired by either party during the marriage, including the increase in value, prior to the date of final separation, of any nonmarital property acquired pursuant to paragraphs (1) and (3), except:

(1) Property acquired prior to marriage or property acquired in exchange for property acquired prior to the marriage.

(2) Property excluded by valid agreement of the parties entered into before, during or after the marriage.

(3) Property acquired by gift, except between spouses, bequest, devise or descent.

(4) Property acquired after final separation until the date of divorce, except for property acquired in exchange for marital assets.

(5) Property which a party has sold, granted, conveyed or otherwise disposed of in good faith and for value prior to the date of final separation.

(6) Veterans' benefits exempt from attachment, levy or seizure pursuant to the act of September 2, 1958 (Public Law 85-857, 72 Stat. 1229), as amended, except for those benefits received by a veteran where the veteran has waived a portion of his military retirement pay in order to receive veterans' compensation.

(7) Property to the extent to which the property has been mortgaged or otherwise encumbered in good faith for value prior to the date of final separation.

(8) Any payment received as a result of an award or settlement for any cause of action or claim which accrued prior to the marriage or after the date of final separation regardless of when payment was received.

(b) **Presumption.**—All real or personal property acquired by either party during the marriage is presumed to be marital property regardless of whether title is held individually or by the parties in some form of co-ownership such as joint tenancy, tenancy in common or tenancy by the entirety. The presumption of marital property is overcome by a showing that the property was acquired by a method listed in subsection (a).

§ 3502. Equitable division of marital property

(a) **General rule.**—In an action for divorce or annulment, the court shall, upon request of either party, equitably divide, distribute or assign, in kind or otherwise, the marital property between the parties without regard to marital misconduct in such proportions and in such manner as the court deems just after considering all relevant factors, including:

(1) The length of the marriage.

(2) Any prior marriage of either party.

(3) The age, health, station, amount and sources of income, vocational skills, employability, estate, liabilities and needs of each of the parties.

(4) The contribution by one party to the education, training or increased earning power of the other party.

(5) The opportunity of each party for future acquisitions of capital assets and income.

(6) The sources of income of both parties, including, but not limited to, medical, retirement, insurance or other benefits.

(7) The contribution or dissipation of each party in the acquisition, preservation, depreciation or appreciation of the marital property, including the contribution of a party as homemaker.

(8) The value of the property set apart to each party.

    (9) The standard of living of the parties established during the marriage.

   (10) The economic circumstances of each party, including Federal, State and local tax ramifications, at the time the division of property is to become effective.

   (11) Whether the party will be serving as the custodian of any dependent minor children.

  (b) **Lien.**—The court may impose a lien or charge upon property of a party as security for the payment of alimony or any other award for the other party.

  (c) **Family home.**—The court may award, during the pendency of the action or otherwise, to one or both of the parties the right to reside in the marital residence.

  (d) **Life insurance.**—The court may direct the continued maintenance and beneficiary designations of existing policies insuring the life or health of either party which were originally purchased during the marriage and owned by or within the effective control of either party. Where it is necessary to protect the interests of a party, the court may also direct the purchase of, and beneficiary designations on, a policy insuring the life or health of either party.

  (e) **Powers of the court.**—If, at any time, a party has failed to comply with an order of equitable distribution, as provided for in this chapter or with the terms of an agreement as entered into between the parties, after hearing, the court may, in addition to any other remedy available under this part, in order to effect compliance with its order:

    (1) enter judgment;

    (2) authorize the taking and seizure of the goods and chattels and collection of the rents and profits of the real and personal, tangible and intangible property of the party;

    (3) award interest on unpaid installments;

    (4) order and direct the transfer or sale of any property required in order to comply with the court's order;

    (5) require security to insure future payments in compliance with the court's order;

    (6) issue attachment proceedings, directed to the sheriff or other proper officer of the county, directing that the person named as having failed to comply with the court order be brought before the court, at such time as the court may direct. If the court finds, after hearing, that the person willfully failed to comply with the court order, it may deem the person in civil contempt of court and, in its discretion, make an appropriate order, including, but not limited to, commitment of the person to the county jail for a period not to exceed six months;

    (7) award counsel fees and costs;

    (8) attach wages; or

    (9) find the party in contempt.

CHAPTER 37

ALIMONY AND SUPPORT

§ 3701. **Alimony**

  (a) **General rule.**—Where a divorce decree has been entered, the court may allow alimony, as it deems reasonable, to either party only if it finds that alimony is necessary.

  (b) **Factors relevant.**—In determining whether alimony is necessary and in determining the nature, amount, duration and manner of payment of alimony, the court shall consider all relevant factors, including:

    (1) The relative earnings and earning capacities of the parties.

    (2) The ages and the physical, mental and emotional conditions of the parties.

    (3) The sources of income of both parties, including, but not limited to, medical, retirement, and insurance or other benefits.

    (4) The expectancies and inheritances of the parties.

(5) The duration of the marriage.

(6) The contribution by one party to the education, training or increased earning power of the other party.

(7) The extent to which the earning power, expenses or financial obligations of a party will be affected by reason of serving as a custodian of a minor child.

(8) The standard of living of the parties established during the marriage.

(9) The relative education of the parties and the time necessary to acquire sufficient education or training to enable the party seeking alimony to find appropriate employment.

(10) The relative assets and liabilities of the parties.

(11) The property brought to the marriage by either party.

(12) The contribution of a spouse as homemaker.

(13) The relative needs of the parties.

(14) The marital misconduct of either of the parties during the marriage. The marital misconduct of either of the parties from the date of final separation shall not be considered by the court in its determinations relative to alimony.

(15) The Federal, State and local tax ramifications of the alimony award.

(16) Whether the party seeking alimony lacks sufficient property, including, but not limited to, property distributed under Chapter 35 (relating to property rights), to provide for the party's reasonable needs.

(17) Whether the party seeking alimony is incapable of self-support through appropriate employment.

   (c)   Duration.—The court in ordering alimony shall determine the duration of the order, which may be for a definite or an indefinite period of time which is reasonable under the circumstances.

   (d)   Statement of reasons.—In an order made under this section, the court shall set forth the reason for its denial or award of alimony and the amount thereof.

   (e)   Modification and termination.—An order entered pursuant to this section is subject to further order of the court upon changed circumstances of either party of a substantial and continuing nature whereupon the order may be modified, suspended, terminated or reinstituted or a new order made. Any further order shall apply only to payments accruing subsequent to the petition for the requested relief. Remarriage of the party receiving alimony shall terminate the award of alimony.

   (f)   Status of agreement to pay alimony.—Whenever the court approves an agreement for the payment of alimony voluntarily entered into between the parties, the agreement shall constitute the order of the court and may be enforced as provided in section 3703 (relating to enforcement of arrearages).

§ 3702.   Alimony pendente lite, counsel fees and expenses

In proper cases, upon petition, the court may allow a spouse reasonable alimony pendente lite, spousal support and reasonable counsel fees and expenses. Reasonable counsel fees and expenses may be allowed pendente lite, and the court shall also have authority to direct that adequate health and hospitalization insurance coverage be maintained for the dependent spouse pendente lite.

§ 3706.   Bar to alimony

No petitioner is entitled to receive an award of alimony where the petitioner, subsequent to the divorce pursuant to which alimony is being sought, has entered into cohabitation with a person of the opposite sex who is not a member of the family of the petitioner within the degrees of consanguinity.

§ 4324.   Inclusion of spousal medical support

In addition to periodic support payments, the court may require that an obligor pay a designated percentage of a spouse's reasonable and necessary health care expenses. If health care coverage is available through an obligor or obligee at no cost as a benefit of employment or at a reasonable cost, the court shall order an obligor or obligee to provide or extend health care coverage to a spouse. Upon failure of the obligor to make this payment or reimburse the spouse and after compliance with procedural due process requirement, the court shall treat the amount as arrearages.

§ 4326. **Mandatory inclusion of child medical support**

(a) **General rule.**—In every proceeding to establish or modify an order which requires the payment of child support, the court shall ascertain the ability of each parent to provide health care coverage for the children of the parties.

(b) **Noncustodial parent requirement.**—If health care coverage is available at a reasonable cost to a non-custodial parent on an employment-related or other group basis, the court shall require that the noncustodial parent provide such coverage to the children of the parties. In cases where there are two noncustodial parents having such coverage available, the court shall require one or both parents to provide coverage.

(c) **Custodial parent coverage.**—If health care coverage is available at a reasonable cost to a custodial parent on an employment-related or other group basis, the court shall require that the custodial parent provide such coverage to the children of the parties, unless adequate health care coverage has already been provided through the noncustodial parent. In cases where the parents have shared custody of the child and coverage is available to both, the court shall require one or both parents to provide coverage, taking into account the financial ability of the parties and the extent of coverage available to each parent.

(d) **Additional requirement.**—If the court finds that health care coverage is not available to either parent at a reasonable cost on an employment-related or other group basis, the court shall order either parent or both parents to obtain for the parties' children health insurance coverage which is available at reasonable cost.

(e) **Uninsured expenses.**—The court shall determine the amount of any deductible and copayments which each parent shall pay. In addition, the court may require that either parent or both parents pay a designated percentage of the reasonable and necessary uncovered health care expenses of the parties' children, including birth-related expenses incurred prior to the filing of the complaint.

(f) **Proof of insurance.**—Within 30 days after the entry of an order requiring a parent to provide health care coverage for a child, the obligated parent shall submit to the other parent, or person having custody of the child, written proof that health care coverage has been obtained or that application for coverage has been made. Proof of coverage shall consist of at a minimum:

(1) The name of the health care coverage provider.

(2) Any applicable identification numbers.

(3) Any cards evidencing coverage.

(4) The address to which claims should be made.

(5) A description of any restrictions on usage, such as prior approval for hospital admissions, and the manner of obtaining approval.

(6) A copy of the benefit booklet or coverage contract.

(7) A description of all deductibles and copayments.

(8) Five copies of any claim forms.

[subsections (g), (h), (h.1), (i), (j), and (k) omitted]

(l) **Definitions.**—As used in this section, the following words and phrases have the meanings given to them in this subsection:

"Child." A child to whom a duty of coverage is owed.

"Health care coverage." Coverage for medical, dental, orthodontic, optical, psychological, psychiatric or other health care services for a child. For the purpose of this section, medical assistance under Subarticle (f) of

Article IV of the act of June 13, 1967 (P.L. 31, No. 21), known as the Public Welfare Code, shall not be considered health care coverage.

"Insurer." A corporation or person incorporated or doing business in this Commonwealth by virtue of the act of May 17, 1921 (P.L. 682, No. 284), known as The Insurance Company Law of 1921; a hospital plan corporation as defined in 40 Pa.C.S. Ch. 61 (relating to hospital plan corporations); a professional health services plan corporation as defined in 40 Pa.C.S. Ch. 63 (relating to professional health services plan corporations); a beneficial society subject to 40 Pa.C.S. Ch. 65 (relating to fraternal benefit societies); a health maintenance organization; or any other person, association, partnership, common-law trust, joint stock company, nonprofit corporation, profit corporation or other entity conducting an insurance business.

"Medical child support order." An order which relates to the child's right to receive certain health care coverage and which:

    (1)   includes the name and last known mailing address of the parent providing health care coverage and the name and last know mailing address of the child;

    (2)   includes a reasonable description of the type of coverage to be provided or includes the manner in which coverage is to be determined;

    (3)   designates the time period to which the order applies;

    (4)   if coverage is provided through a group health plan, designates each plan to which the order applies; and

    (5)   includes the name and address of the custodial parent.

§ 4327. Postsecondary educational costs

    (a)   General rule.—Where applicable under this section, a court may order either or both parents who are separated, divorced, unmarried or otherwise subject to an existing support obligation to provide equitably for educational costs of their child whether an application for this support is made before or after the child has reached 18 years of age. The responsibility to provide for postsecondary educational expenses is a shared responsibility between both parents. The duty of a parent to provide a postsecondary education for a child is not as exacting a requirement as the duty to provide food, clothing and shelter for a child of tender years unable to support himself. This authority shall extend to postsecondary education, including periods of undergraduate or vocational education after the child graduates from high school. An award for postsecondary educational costs may be entered only after the child or student has made reasonable efforts to apply for scholarships, grants and work-study assistance.

    (b)   Action to recover educational expenses.—An action to recover educational costs may be commenced:

    (1)   by the student if over 18 years of age; or

    (2)   by either parent on behalf of a child under 18 years of age, but, if the student is over 18 years of age, the student's written consent to the action must be secured.

    (c)   Calculation of educational costs.—In making an award under this section, the court shall calculate educational costs as defined in this section.

    (d)   Grants and scholarships.—The court shall deduct from the educational costs all grants and scholarships awarded to the student.

    (e)   Other relevant factors.—After calculating educational costs and deducting grants and scholarships, the court may order either parent or both parents to pay all or part of the remaining educational costs of their child. The court shall consider all relevant factors which appear reasonable, equitable and necessary, including the following:

    (1)   The financial resources of both parents.

    (2)   The financial resources of the student.

    (3)   The receipt of educational loans and other financial assistance by the student.

    (4)   The ability, willingness and desire of the student to pursue and complete the course of study.

(5) Any willful estrangement between parent and student caused by the student after attaining majority.

(6) The ability of the student to contribute to the student's expenses through gainful employment. The student's history of employment is material under this paragraph.

(7) Any other relevant factors.

(f) When liability may not be found.—A court shall not order support for educational costs if any of the following circumstances exist:

(1) Undue financial hardship would result to the parent.

(2) The educational costs would be a contribution for post-college graduate educational costs.

(3) The order would extend support for the student beyond the student's twenty-third birthday. If exceptional circumstances exist, the court may order educational support for the student beyond the student's twenty-third birthday.

(g) Parent's obligation.—A parent's obligation to contribute toward the educational costs of a student shall not include payments to the other parent for the student's living expenses at home unless the student resides at home with the other parent and commutes to school.

(h) Termination or modification of orders.—Any party may request modification or termination of an order entered under this section upon proof of change in educational status of the student, a material change in the financial status of any party or other relevant factors.

(i) Applicability.—

(1) This act shall apply to all divorce decrees, support agreements, support orders, agreed or stipulated court orders, property settlement agreements, equitable distribution agreements, custody agreements and/or court orders and agreed to or stipulated court orders in effect on, executed or entered since, November 12, 1992.

(2) In addition, this act shall apply to all pending actions for support. This section shall not supersede or modify the express terms of a voluntary written marital settlement agreement or any court order entered pursuant thereto.

(j) Definitions.—As used in this section, the following words and phrases shall have the meanings given to them in this subsection:

"Educational costs." Tuition, fees, books, room, board and other educational materials.

"Postsecondary education." An educational or vocational program provided at a college, university or other postsecondary vocational, secretarial, business or technical school.

CHAPTER 53

CUSTODY

§ 5303. Award of custody, partial custody or visitation

(a) General rule.—In making an order for custody, partial custody or visitation to either parent, the court shall consider, among other factors, which parent is more likely to encourage, permit and allow frequent and continuing contact and physical access between the noncustodial parent and the child. In addition, the court shall consider each parent and adult household member's present and past violent or abusive conduct which may include, but is not limited to, abusive conduct as defined under the act of October 7, 1976 (P.L. 1090, No. 218), known as the Protection From Abuse Act.

§ 5304. Award of shared custody

An order for shared custody may be awarded by the court when it is in the best interest of the child:

(1) upon application of one or both parents;

(2) when the parties have agreed to an award of shared custody; or

(3) in the discretion of the court.

APPENDIX B
CHECKLISTS

This appendix contains basic checklists of the forms you will most likely need to prepare for the type of divorce procedure you select. The purpose of these checklists is to help you be sure that you have prepared all of the forms necessary. Of course, once you visit your prothonotary's office (or clerk's office), you may determine that you need additional or different forms that are required by your county. You may find at least one blank line at the end of each section of the various checklists, which can be used to add in any of these other forms.

The following checklists are included in this appendix:

CHECKLIST 1: MUTUAL CONSENT DIVORCE — MOST COUNTIES

Initial Documents:

- ☐ Civil Cover Sheet (form 13)
- ☐ Notice to Defend and Claim Rights (form 3)
- ☐ Complaint in Divorce (form 4)
- ☐ Affidavit (form 5), stapled to Complaint in Divorce
- ☐ Court of Common Pleas Intake (form 6)
- ☐ Domestic Relations Income and Expense Statement (form 7)
- ☐ Notice to File Social Security Numbers (form 23)
- ☐ _____
- ☐ _____

After Ninety Days:

- ☐ Marital Property Settlement Agreement (form 9)
- ☐ Acknowledgment (form 10) signed by you, and stapled to Marital Property Settlement Agreement
- ☐ Acknowledgment (form 10) signed by your spouse, and stapled to Marital Property Settlement Agreement
- ☐ Affidavit of Consent (form 16), signed by you
- ☐ Affidavit of Consent (form 17), signed by your spouse
- ☐ Support Guideline Computations—Child Support (form 8), if you have minor children
- ☐ Praecipe to Transmit Record (form 12)
- ☐ Decree of Divorce (form 18)
- ☐ Record of Divorce or Annulment (form 20), commonly called the "vital statistics form"
- ☐ Notice of Intention to Retake Prior Name (form 24), if you are the wife and desire to resume using a former name.
- ☐ _____
- ☐ _____

CHECKLIST 2: MUTUAL CONSENT DIVORCE — PHILADELPHIA COUNTY

Initial Documents:

☐ Domestic Relations Information Sheet (form 25)

☐ Complaint in Divorce (form 26)

☐ _____

☐ _____

☐ _____

After Ninety Days:

☐ Marital Property Settlement Agreement (form 33)

☐ Acknowledgment (form 10, or a similar form if you are required to use one obtained from the clerk) signed by you, and stapled to Marital Property Settlement Agreement

☐ Acknowledgment (form 10, or a similar form if you are required to use one obtained from the clerk) signed by your spouse, and stapled to Marital Property Settlement Agreement

☐ Waiver of Notice of Intention to Request Entry of Divorce Under § 3301(c) of the Divorce Code (form 30), signed by you

☐ Notice of Intention to Request Entry of §3301(c) Divorce Decree (form 31) [if your spouse is **not** represented by an attorney]; or Notice of Intention to Request Entry of Divorce (Cases Under Section 3301(c) of the Divorce Code) (form 32) [if your spouse **is** represented by an attorney]; signed by you.

☐ Praecipe to Transmit Record (form 27)

☐ Decree (obtain form from the Family Court Clerk)

☐ Record of Divorce or Annulment (form 20), commonly called the "vital statistics form"

☐ Notice of Intention to Retake Prior Name (form 24), if you are the wife and desire to resume using a former name.

☐ _____

☐ _____

☐ _____

CHECKLIST 3: STANDARD UNCONTESTED DIVORCE — MOST COUNTIES

Initial Documents:

☐ Civil Cover Sheet (form 13).

☐ Notice to Defend and Claim Rights (form 3).

☐ Complaint in Divorce (form 4).

☐ Affidavit (form 5), stapled to the Complaint in Divorce

☐ Court of Common Pleas Intake (form 6).

☐ Domestic Relations Income and Expense Statement (form 7).

☐ _____

☐ _____

Documents to Conclude Case:

☐ Support Guideline Computations—Child Support (form 8), if you and your spouse have any minor children.

☐ Notice of Intention to Request Entry of Divorce Decree (form 21)

☐ Praecipe to Transmit Record (form 12).

☐ Notice to File Social Security Numbers (form 23).

☐ Decree of Divorce (form 18).

☐ Record of Divorce or Annulment (form 20).

☐ Notice of Intention to Retake Prior Name (form 24), if you are the wife and desire to resume using a former name.

☐ _____

☐ _____

If Agreement Reached:

☐ Marital Property Settlement Agreement (form 9)

☐ Acknowledgment (form 10) signed by you, and stapled to Marital Property Settlement Agreement

☐ Acknowledgment (form 10) signed by your spouse, and stapled to Marital Property Settlement Agreement

☐ Affidavit of Consent (form 16) signed by you

☐ Affidavit of Consent (form 17) signed by your spouse

☐ _____

CHECKLIST 4: STANDARD UNCONTESTED DIVORCE — PHILADELPHIA COUNTY

Initial Documents:

☐ Domestic Relations Information Sheet (form 25)

☐ Complaint in Divorce (form 26).

☐ Plaintiff's Affidavit (form 27)

☐ _____

Documents to Conclude Case:

☐ Notice of Intention to Request Entry of § 3301(d) Divorce Decree (form 35) [if your spouse is ***not*** represented by an attorney]; or Notice of Intention to Request Entry of Divorce (Cases Under Section 3301(c) of the Divorce Code) (form 34) [if your spouse ***is*** represented by an attorney]

☐ Praecipe to Transmit Record (form 28).

☐ Decree. You will need to obtain the appropriate decree form from the Family Court Clerk. There are two decree forms for use in a divorce under Section 3301(d); one (titled "Decree") for cases without a Marital Property Settlement Agreement, and one (titled "Decree and Order") for cases with a Marital Property Settlement Agreement.

☐ Record of Divorce or Annulment (form 20), commonly called the "vital statistics form."

☐ Notice of Intention to Retake Prior Name (form 24), if you are the wife and desire to resume using a former name.

☐ _____

If Agreement Reached:

☐ Marital Property Settlement Agreement (form 33)

☐ Acknowledgment (form 10, or a similar form if you are required to use a form obtained from the clerk) signed by you, and stapled to Marital Property Settlement Agreement

☐ Acknowledgment (form 10, or a similar form if you are required to use a form obtained from the clerk) signed by your spouse, and stapled to Marital Property Settlement Agreement

☐ Waiver of Notice of Intention to Request Entry of a Divorce Decree Under § 3301(c) of the Divorce Code (form 30), signed by the plaintiff (you).

☐ Waiver of Notice of Intention to Request Entry of a Divorce Decree Under § 3301(c) of the Divorce Code (form 30), signed by the defendant (your spouse).

☐ _____

CHECKLIST 5: CONTESTED DIVORCE — MOST COUNTIES

Initial Documents:

☐ Civil Cover Sheet (form 13).

☐ Notice to Defend and Claim Rights (form 3).

☐ Complaint in Divorce (form 4).

☐ Affidavit (form 5), stapled to the Complaint in Divorce

☐ Court of Common Pleas Intake (form 6)

☐ Domestic Relations Income and Expense Statement (form 7)

☐ _____

Documents to Conclude Case:

☐ Support Guideline Computations - Child Support (form 8), if you and your spouse have any minor children.

☐ Notice of Intention to Request Entry of Divorce Decree (form 21) and Counteraffidavit Under § 3301(d) of the Divorce Code (form 22). Both of these forms must be filed after your spouse is served with the Complaint in Divorce, and before submission of the final documents necessary to conclude the divorce. Both of these forms must be served on your spouse and filed with the Office of the Prothonotary.

☐ Praecipe to Transmit Record (form 12).

☐ Notice to File Social Security Numbers (form 23).

☐ Decree of Divorce (form 18).

☐ Record of Divorce or Annulment (form 20).

☐ Notice of Intention to Retake Prior Name (form 24), if you are the wife and desire to resume using a former name.

☐ _____

If Agreement Reached:

☐ Marital Property Settlement Agreement (form 9)

☐ Acknowledgment (form 10) signed by you, and stapled to Marital Property Settlement Agreement

☐ Acknowledgment (form 10) signed by your spouse, and stapled to Marital Property Settlement Agreement

☐ Affidavit of Consent (form 16), signed by you

☐ Affidavit of Consent (form 17), signed by your spouse

CHECKLIST 6: CONTESTED DIVORCE — PHILADELPHIA COUNTY

Initial Documents:

☐ Domestic Relations Information Sheet (form 25)

☐ Complaint in Divorce (form 26).

☐ Plaintiff's Affidavit (form 27)

☐ _____

Documents to Conclude Case:

☐ Notice of Intention to Request Entry of § 3301(d) Divorce Decree (form 35) [if your spouse is **not** represented by an attorney]; or Notice of Intention to Request Entry of Divorce (Cases Under Section 3301(c) of the Divorce Code) (form 34) [if your spouse **is** represented by an attorney]

☐ Praecipe to Transmit Record (form 28).

☐ Decree. You will need to obtain the appropriate decree form from the Family Court Clerk. There are two decree forms for use in a divorce under Section 3301(d); one (titled "Decree") for cases without a Marital Property Settlement Agreement, and one (titled "Decree and Order") for cases with a Marital Property Settlement Agreement.

☐ Record of Divorce or Annulment (form 20), commonly called the "vital statistics form."

☐ Notice of Intention to Retake Prior Name (form 24), if you are the wife and desire to resume using a former name.

☐ _____

If Agreement Reached:

☐ Marital Property Settlement Agreement (form 33)

☐ Acknowledgment (form 10, or a similar form if you are required to use a form obtained from the clerk) signed by you, and stapled to Marital Property Settlement Agreement

☐ Acknowledgment (form 10, or a similar form if you are required to use a form obtained from the clerk) signed by your spouse, and stapled to Marital Property Settlement Agreement

☐ Waiver of Notice of Intention to Request Entry of a Divorce Decree Under § 3301(d) of the Divorce Code (form 30), signed by the plaintiff.

☐ Waiver of Notice of Intention to Request Entry of a Divorce Decree Under § 3301(c) of the Divorce Code (form 30), signed by the defendant.

☐ _____

Appendix C
Blank Forms

Be sure to read the section "An Introduction to Legal Forms" in Chapter 5 before you begin using the forms in this appendix. The pages in the text containing instructions for a particular form may be found by looking in the index. Instead of removing forms, it is suggested that you make photocopies to use for both practice worksheets and the forms you will file with the court. The blank forms can then be used to make more copies in the event you make mistakes or need additional copies. The forms in this appendix are not in any particular order, and you may not need to use all of the forms.

Philadelphia Forms. Philadelphia County requires the use of its own forms. The best way for you to be sure the forms you prepare will be acceptable to the court is to obtain the forms from the clerk of the Domestic Relations Division of the Family Division of the Court of Common Pleas (located at 34 South 11th Street, Philadelphia, PA 19107). Although the forms you will get will most likely be very poor quality photocopies, they will most likely be accepted without question by the clerk. The clerk's office can also provide you with its latest written instructions on the filing procedure. Forms 25 through 36 in this appendix are recreations of Philadelphia County forms, however, these may not be acceptable to the court clerk.

TABLE OF FORMS

The forms listed below are contained in this appendix. The form number may be found in the upper, outside corner of the first page of each form. Also listed is the page on which each form begins. Forms 1 through 24 are general forms for use in most Pennsylvania counties. Forms 25 through 36 are recreations of these forms used in Philadelphia County.

If you are filing in Philadelphia County, check forms 25-36 before using forms 1-24 to see if there is a Philadelphia-specific form.

Special Note on Philadelphia Forms

If you will be filing your divorce case in Philadelphia County, you will find that the court there is very particular about how things must be done and has its own required forms. In Appendix C you will find some forms that are required in Philadelphia. When the authors requested forms from the Philadelphia family court clerk's office, we received many forms of very poor quality.

Some of these forms also contain errors, such as one which refers to grounds for divorce as a "Three (2) Year Separation Where the Court Determines That There is a Reasonable Prospect of Reconciliation." The correct grounds are a *two* year separation where the court finds there is *no* reasonable prospect of reconciliation. Therefore, we recreated these forms in much better quality for Appendix C. However, there is no guarantee that the Philadelphia family court clerk will accept the forms from Appendix C, and you may find that you need to obtain the forms from the Philadelphia family court clerk's office.

General Forms:

Philadelphia County Forms:

PROPERTY INVENTORY

N	Amount	Property	Assigned To Whom	Misc. Info.	Current Value

Name: _____

Day: _____ Date: _____

Total: $ _____ Total: $ _____

Property Value Debt Amount

DEBT INVENTORY

N	Amount	Debt	Assigned To Whom	Misc. Info.	Current Balance

Name: _____

Day: _____   Date: _____

Total: $ _____   Total: $ _____

         Property Value   Debt Amount

_____   (IN THE COURT OF COMMON PLEAS OF

       PLAINTIFF,   (

                    (_____COUNTY, PENNSYLVANIA

    v.   (

                    (CIVIL DIVISION

                    (

_____   (NO:

       DEFENDANT.

NOTICE TO DEFEND AND CLAIM RIGHTS

YOU HAVE BEEN SUED IN COURT. IF YOU WISH TO DEFEND AGAINST THE CLAIM SET FORTH IN THE FOLLOWING PAGES, YOU MUST TAKE PROMPT ACTION. YOU ARE WARNED THAT IF YOU FAIL TO DO SO, THE CASE MAY PROCEED WITHOUT YOU AND A DECREE OF DIVORCE OR ANNULMENT MAY BE ENTERED AGAINST YOU BY THE COURT. A JUDGMENT MAY ALSO BE ENTERED AGAINST YOU FOR ANY OTHER CLAIM OR RELIEF REQUESTED IN THESE PAPERS BY THE PLAINTIFF. YOU MAY LOSE MONEY OR PROPERTY OR OTHER RIGHTS IMPORTANT TO YOU, INCLUDING CUSTODY OR VISITATION OF YOUR CHILD(REN).

WHEN THE GROUND FOR THE DIVORCE ARE INDIGNITIES OR IRRETRIEVABLE BREAKDOWN OF THE MARRIAGE, YOU MAY REQUEST MARRIAGE COUNSELING. A LIST OF MARRIAGE COUNSELORS IS AVAILABLE IN THE OFFICE OF THE PROTHONOTARY AT _____ _____, PENNSYLVANIA.

IF YOU DO NOT FILE A CLAIM FOR ALIMONY, DIVISION OF PROPERTY, LAWYERS FEES, OR EXPENSES BEFORE A DIVORCE OR ANNULMENT IS GRANTED, YOU MAY LOSE THE RIGHT TO CLAIM ANY OF THEM

YOU SHOULD TAKE THIS PAPER TO YOUR LAWYER AT ONCE. IF YOU DO NOT HAVE A LAWYER OR CANNOT AFFORD ONE, GO TO OR TELEPHONE THE OFFICE SET FORTH BELOW TO FIND OUT WHERE YOU CAN GET LEGAL HELP.

LAWYERS REFERRAL SERVICE

_____

_____

Telephone: _____

_____

For Petitioner

Address: _____

_____

Telephone: _____

_____   (IN THE COURT OF COMMON PLEAS OF

                  PLAINTIFF,   (

                           (_____COUNTY, PENNSYLVANIA

           v.   (

                       (CIVIL DIVISION

                       (

_____   (NO:

                DEFENDANT.

COMPLAINT IN DIVORCE

     AND NOW COMES, the Petitioner, _____, by FILING PRO SE, who files this Complaint in Divorce a statement of which is as follow:

1.   The Petitioner is _____, an adult individual currently residing at _____.

2.   The Defendant is _____, an adult individual currently residing at _____ .

3.   The Petitioner has been a bona fide resident of the Commonwealth of Pennsylvania for at least six (6) months previous to the filing of this Complaint.

4.   The Petitioner and Respondent were married on date:_____ in the State of _____.

5.   There (is) are _____ child(ren) born of this marriage. Name(s)_____

       _____ Birthdate(s):_____

6.   Neither party is a member of any branch of military.

7.   The marriage is irretrievably broken.

8.   The Petitioner, _____, respectfully requests this Honorable Court to a grant this Divorce pursuant to Section 3301 (c), or in the alternative, Section 3301 (d) of the Divorce Code.

                      Respectfully submitted,

                      _____

                      Name: _____

                      Full Address: _____

                      _____

                      Telephone: _____

     I verify that the statements made in the Complaint are true and correct. I understand that false statements made herein are subject to penalties of 18 Pa. C.S.A. Section 4904, relating to unsworn falsification to authorities.

Dated: _____   _____

_____   (IN THE COURT OF COMMON PLEAS OF

                PLAINTIFF,   (

                              (_____COUNTY, PENNSYLVANIA

           v.   (

                           (CIVIL DIVISION

                           (

_____   (NO:

             DEFENDANT.

AFFIDAVIT

COMMONWEALTH OF PENNSYLVANIA   )

) ss:

COUNTY OF:)

      Before me, the subscriber, a Notary Public in and for said Commonwealth and County, personally appeared _____, who being duly sworn according to law, deposes and says that the facts contained within the foregoing Complaint in Divorce are true and correct to the best of his/her knowledge, information, and belief, and that he/she is authorized to make this Affidavit.

_____

                   Name

Sworn to and subscribed before me this

_____ day of _____, 200____.

_____

NOTARY PUBLIC

COUNTY COURT OF COMMON PLEAS

INTAKE

THIS FORM MUST BE FILLED OUT IF YOU ARE FILING A DIVORCE OR CUSTODY ACTION IN THE PROTHONOTARY'S OFFICE:

TODAY'S DATE: _____

CASE NUMBER: _____

PLEASE CHECK ONE:

      □   DIVORCE FILING — NO CHILDREN:

      □   DIVORCE FILING — W/CHILDREN UNDER 18:

      □   CUSTODY FILING — W/CHILDREN UNDER 18:

PLAINTIFF/PETITIONER NAME AND ADDRESS:

DEFENDANT/RESPONDENT NAME AND ADDRESS:

REQUIRED INFORMATION   TODAY'S DATE _____

Plaintiff/Defendant

_____ **County Domestic Relations Department**

Income and Expense Statement

Name _____

Date of Birth _____ SS# _____ Phone # _____

Home Address _____

Drivers License # _____

Employer _____ Position _____

Address _____

Phone _____ Date Employed _____

Other Employment _____

Health Insurance Company Name _____ Policy # _____

Address_____ Group # _____

1. Check Method of Payment and List Gross Income:

   Paid: ☐ Every 2 weeks   ☐ Twice Monthly   ☐ Monthly   ☐ Weekly $_____

                                                                              Gross Income

2. Subtract tax deductions:

   Federal Income Tax $ _____

   Social Security   _____

   State Income Tax   _____

   Local Income Tax   _____

   Health Insurance   _____

   Union Dues   _____

   Pension Contributions _____

   Credit Union   _____

   Other Deductions   _____

   Total Deductions   _____   -$_____

              Subtract Totals from Gross Income

                                                              _____

                                                              NET INCOME

<u>ALL OTHER INCOME</u>

List any interest and dividends, pensions and annuity, Social Security, net income from property, Unemployment Compensation, Workmen's Compensation or other, such as royalties, expense accounts, gifts, etc. (if no other income check none)   NONE ☐

_____ $ _____

_____   _____

_____   _____

Total Other Income   _____

Deduct Estimated Income Taxes on such Other Income   _____

Final Net Income Per Week $ _____

_____ **COUNTY**

D.R.S.

Docket _____   Date _____

Defendant _____   C.O. _____

Plaintiff _____

Rule 1910.16-3 Support Guidelines Formula

    (a) The formula for the determination of the amount of support is as follows:

SUPPORT GUIDELINE COMPUTATIONS
CHILD SUPPORT

		DEFENDANT	PLAINTIFF
1.	Total Gross Income Per Pay Period	_____	_____
2.	Net Income	_____	_____
3.	Conversion to Monthly Amount	_____	_____
4.	COMBINE INCOME OF BOTH DEFENDANT AND PLAINTIFF		_____
5.	Proportionate Expenditure (determined from chart)		x _____ %
6.	Basic Child Support (multiply #4 by #5)		= _____
7.	Additional support if required		_____
8.	Total Support		_____
9.	Percentage of each parent's obligation (divide line #3 by #4)	_____ %	_____ %
10.	Each parent's obligation	$ _____	$ _____

SPOUSAL SUPPORT WITH DEPENDENT CHILDREN

11.	DEFENDANT'S MONTHLY NET INCOME	$ _____
12.	LESS PLAINTIFF'S MONTHLY NET INCOME	- $ _____
13.	DIFFERENCE	$ _____
14.	LESS DEFENDANT'S CHILD SUPPORT OBLIGATION	- $ _____
15	DIFFERENCE	$ _____
16.	MULTIPLY BY 30%	_____ .30
17.	AMOUNT OF MONTHLY SPOUSAL SUPPORT	$ _____

18. COMBINE SPOUSAL SUPPORT (line 17) AND CHILD SUPPORT FOR A TOTAL SUPPORT AWARD.

SPOUSAL SUPPORT WITHOUT DEPENDENT CHILDREN

19.	DEFENDANT'S MONTHLY NET INCOME (line #3)	$ _____
20.	LESS PLAINTIFF'S MONTHLY INCOME (line #3)	- $ _____
21.	DIFFERENCE	$ _____
22.	MULTIPLY BY 40%	x _____ .40
23.	AMOUNT OF MONTHLY SPOUSAL SUPPORT	$ _____

RULE 1910.16-3 DRS 10/92

```
_____      ( IN THE COURT OF COMMON PLEAS OF
                   PLAINTIFF,      (
                                   ( _____COUNTY, PENNSYLVANIA
          v.                       (
                                   ( CIVIL DIVISION
                                   (
_____      ( NO:
                  DEFENDANT.
```

MARITAL PROPERTY SETTLEMENT AGREEMENT

THIS AGREEMENT, made this _____ day of _____, 200____, between

PLAINTIFF, _____, residing at _____,

(city) _____, Pennsylvania _____ *(zip)*, hereinafter

called "Husband" / "Wife," and

DEFENDANT, _____, residing at _____,

(city) _____, Pennsylvania _____ *(zip)*, hereinafter

called "Husband" / "Wife."

WITNESSETH

WHEREAS, the parties were married on: (date) _____;

WHEREAS, the parties filed for 3301(c) Divorce on: (date) _____;

WHEREAS, the parties hereto desire to settle their property rights;

WHEREAS, both parties agree to relinquish any and all claims which either may have against any property now owned or belonging to the other or which may hereinafter be acquired by either of them by purchase, gift, devise, bequest, inheritance, or otherwise, except as to the obligations, covenants, and agreements contained herein; and

WHEREAS, both parties each have had opportunity to seek the benefit of competent and independent legal advise by separate counsel.

NOW, THEREFORE, the parties, intending to be legally bound, do covenant and agree as follows:

1. INCORPORATION OF RECITALS

The recitals on Page 1 of this Agreement are incorporated herein as if set forth in full. Each paragraph hereof shall be deemed to be a separate and independent covenant and agreement.

2. APPLICABLE LAW

This Agreement shall be construed under the laws of the Commonwealth of Pennsylvania.

3. PROPERTY TO BE RETAINED BY WIFE.

Husband and Wife agree that, unless otherwise indicated in this agreement, the Wife shall keep all of her own personal clothing and effects; and that the following property shall also be retained by the Wife:

4. PROPERTY TO BE RETAINED BY HUSBAND.

Husband and Wife agree that, unless otherwise indicated in this agreement, the Husband shall keep all of his own personal clothing and effects, and that the following property shall also be retained by the Husband:

5. DEBTS TO BE PAID BY WIFE.

Husband and Wife agree that the Wife shall pay the following debts and will not at any time hold the Husband responsible for them:

6. DEBTS TO BE PAID BY HUSBAND.

Husband and Wife agree that the Husband shall pay the following debts and will not at any time hold the Wife responsible for them:

7. PENSION AND/OR PROFIT SHARING PLANS, BANK ACCOUNTS, STOCKS, BONDS, SECURITIES, CREDIT UNION ACCOUNTS, AND INDIVIDUAL RETIREMENT ACCOUNTS

Husband and Wife distribute the respective accounts as follows:

8. REAL ESTATE

9. ALIMONY, ALIMONY PENDENTE LITE, SPOUSAL SUPPORT, EXPENSES AND ALL MARITAL RIGHTS

Each of the parties hereto release the other from subsequent claims for alimony, alimony pendente lite, or spousal support, except as set forth as follows:

10. JOINT DEBTS

Husband and Wife warrant and certify to each other that there are no individual or joint marital obligations outstanding, other than those listed in paragraphs 5 and 6 above.

11. DIVORCE

Husband and Wife agree that the marriage is irretrievably broken and will proceed with said Divorce under 23 Pa. C.A. Section 3301(c).

12. TAX ADVICE

The transfers set forth herein may result in income, inheritance, estate, and other tax consequences to the parties. The parties specifically acknowledge that no attorney involved in the negotiating or drafting of this Agreement has provided any tax advised regarding the dispositions contained herein. The parties have been advised to seek separate tax counsel concerning the Divorce distributions.

IN WITNESS WHEREOF, the parties have hereunto set their hands and seals the day and year first above written.

_____   _____
Witness   PLAINTIFF

_____   _____
Witness   DEFENDANT

On this _____ day of _____, 200____, before me, a Notary Public, the undersigned officer, personally appeared NAMES _____and
_____, known to me to be the persons whose names are subscribed to the written instrument, and acknowledged that they executed the same for the purposes therein contained.

IN WITNESS WHEREOF, I hereunto set my hand and official seal.

_____

Notary Public

_____   (IN THE COURT OF COMMON PLEAS OF

        PLAINTIFF,   (

                    (_____COUNTY, PENNSYLVANIA

     v.   (

                    (CIVIL DIVISION

                    (

_____   (NO:

        DEFENDANT.

<u>ACKNOWLEDGEMENT</u>

A complaint in Divorce under Section 3301 (c) of the Divorce Code was filed on _____/_____/_____. I agree that the marriage of the Plaintiff and Defendant is irretrievably broken and ninety days have elapsed from the date of filing the Complaint. All information contained within the attached documentation is true and correct to the best of my knowledge, information, and belief.

It is my desire to file with the _____ County Court of Common Pleas the attached Marital Property Settlement Agreement and to be bound fully and completely by the terms and conditions as set forth within said Marital Property Settlement Agreement documentation.

IN WITNESS WHEREOF, I set my hand and seal this _____ day of _____, 200_____.

_____

NAME:

On this _____ day of _____, 200_____, before me, a Notary Public, the undersigned officer, personally appeared NAME _____, known to me to be the person whose name is subscribed to the written instrument, and acknowledged that she executed the same for the purposes therein contained.

IN WITNESS WHEREOF, I hereunto set my hand and official seal.

_____

Notary Public

	(IN THE COURT OF COMMON PLEAS OF
_____	(
PLAINTIFF,	(
	(_____COUNTY, PENNSYLVANIA
v.	(
	(CIVIL DIVISION
	(
_____	(NO:
DEFENDANT.	

CERTIFICATE (Proof) OF SERVICE

PLAINTIFF NAME: _____ of the Commonwealth of Pennsylvania, hereby affirms the following statement under penalty of perjury:

1.   I am the plaintiff in this action. I hereby certify that on _____, 200___ (DATE), I caused a copy of the attached:

NAME OF DOCUMENT: _____

to be served upon

Defendant's NAME: _____

ADDRESS: _____

by depositing a true copy of same enclosed in a post-paid properly addressed wrapper, in a depository under the exclusive care and custody of the U.S. Postal Service within the Commonwealth of Pennsylvania.

Dated: _____

_____

NAME: _____,

Plaintiff.

_____   (IN THE COURT OF COMMON PLEAS OF

                PLAINTIFF,   (

                       (_____COUNTY, PENNSYLVANIA

           v.   (

                       (CIVIL DIVISION

                       (

_____   (NO:

              DEFENDANT.

PRAECIPE TO TRANSMIT RECORD

To the Prothonotary:

      Kindly Transmit the Record, together with the following information, to the Court for entry of a divorce decree:

      1.   Ground for Divorce: irretrievable breakdown under Section 3301 (c) or 3301 (d) of the Divorce Code. (Strike out applicable section.)

      2.   Date and manner of service of the Complaint: on or about GIVE DATE: _____ via (circle one) Personal Service or Certified Mail.

      3.   (Complete either paragraph (a) or (b).)

      (a) Date of execution of the Affidavit of Consent/Consent Waiver required by Section 3301 (c) of the Divorce Code: by Plaintiff (/   /   ); by Defendant (/   /   ).

      (b) (1) Date of execution of the Plaintiff's Affidavit required by Section 3301 (d) of the Divorce Code:

      (2) Date of service of the Plaintiff's Affidavit required by Section 3301(d) of the Divorce Code:

      4.   Related claims pending: None.

                                     _____

                                   Plaintiff

                                   Address: _____

                                   _____

                                   Phone: (   ) _____

      5.   Date and manner of service of the Notice of Intention to file Praecipe to Transmit Record, a copy of which is attached, if the Decree is to be entered under Section 3301 (d) of the Divorce Code.

_____ COUNTY COURT OF COMMON PLEAS
CIVIL COVER SHEET

Docket No. _____

I (a) PLAINTIFFS	DEFENDANTS
(b) PLAINTIFF'S ATTORNEYS (ADDRESS)	DEFENDANT'S ATTORNEY'S (IF KNOWN) (ADDRESS)

II. MANDATORY ARBITRATION

Does this fall under the mandatory arbitration requirements per Local Rule 1301?

Yes or (No)

III. ALTERNATE DISPUTE RESOLUTION REQUESTED

_____ Summary Jury Trial

_____ Other: See "Guide to Alternate Dispute
Resolution Programs" Published by the
_____County Bar Association

N/A

IV. CAUSE(S) OF ACTION (Cite the statutes or rules of law under which you are filing and write a brief statement of causes(s).)

Divorce Code § 3301 (c) or (d)

V. GENERAL NATURE OF SUIT (Place an X in <u>one area only</u> that most accurately describes your case)

CONTRACT

_____ Insurance
_____ PA Bond
_____ Collection Suits
_____ Construction
_____ Other - List in
         IV above

REAL PROPERTY

_____ Condemnation
_____ Foreclosure
_____ Landlord & Tenant
_____ Partition
_____ Mechanics' Lien
_____ Environment
_____ Other - List
         in IV above
_____ Address of Property _____

PERSONAL INJURY

_____ Motor Vehicle
_____ Product Liability
_____ Medical Malpractice
_____ Other Prof. Liability
_____ Intentional
_____ Premises
_____ Other - List in
         IV above

PRISONER PETITIONS

_____ Habeas Corpus
_____ Mandamus
_____ Other - List in
         IV above

_____ **LABOR**

DOMESTIC RELATIONS

_X_ Divorce
_____ Protection from Abuse
_____ Custody/Visitation
_____ Other - List in IV above
_____ Support

OTHER STATUTES

_____ Zoning Appeal
_____ School Board Appeal
_____ License Suspension Appeal
_____ Assessment Appeal
_____ Other - List in IV above

_____ **TAX LIEN &**
         TAX MATTERS
OTHER
_____ List in IV above

(a) Is this an equity case? Yes or No   (b) Does it involve a governmental body? Yes or No

VI. ORIGIN (Mark only 1)

_X_ 1 Original   ___ 2 Removed from   ___ 3 Confessed   ___ 4 Transferred   ___ 5 Appeal   ___ 6 Appeal to   ___ 7 Foreign
    Complaint   Federal Court   Judgments by   From Another   From   Court from   Judgment
    of Writ   Complaint   District or   Govt.   District
                                                   or Praecipe   County (specify)   Agency   Justice
                                                                                                                 Judgment

VII. REQUESTED IN COMPLAINT   N/A

(a) Is this a CLASS ACTION YES or NO

(c) Amount demanded in complaint _____

(b) Circle YES only if jury demanded in complaint:
    JURY DEMAND: YES or NO
    Will you accept 6 jurors? YES or NO

VIII. RELATED CASE(S) IF ANY   JUDGE _____   DOCKET NUMBER _____

Case Caption

DATE _____

SIGNATURE OF FILING PARTY OR ATTORNEY OF RECORD

IN THE COURT OF COMMON PLEAS

OF _____ COUNTY, PENNSYLVANIA

	:	**CIVIL DIVISION**
_____	:	
Plaintiff	:	No.
	:	
vs.	:	TEMPORARY CUSTODY PETITION
	:	
_____	:	Filed on Behalf of Plaintiff
Defendant	:	
	:	Plaintiff Name and
	:	_____
	:	_____
	:	_____
	:	Phone ( ) _____

PETITION FOR TEMPORARY CUSTODY

AND NOW, comes the petitioner, _____, pro se, and respectfully represents in support of petitioner's complaint that:

1. The petitioner, _____, is an adult individual residing at _____, _____, Pennsylvania _____. This is petitioner's petition for custody.

2. The respondent, _____, is an adult individual residing at _____, _____, Pennsylvania _____.

3. The parties were married on _____/_____/_____, separated on _____/_____/_____.

4. The petitioner seeks custody of the following children, not born out of wedlock:

    Child One, DOB; _____/_____/_____;   Child Two, DOB: _____/_____/_____;

    Child Three, DOB; _____/_____/_____;   Child Four, DOB: _____/_____/_____;

5. The children are presently in the physical custody of _____.

6. State and medical conditions of the children:

7. During the past _____ years, the children have resided with the following persons and at the following addresses:

☐ The children has/have resided with their natural parents all their lives in Pennsylvania.

☐ Other:

8. The natural mother of children is _____, residing at the address above-listed.

9. The natural father of the children is _____, residing at the address above-listed.

10. The Court has jurisdiction to determine the custody of the children because Pennsylvania is the children's home state as defined by PS Section 5344. The children and the parties have significant connection with the Commonwealth and substantial evidence concerning the present and future care, protection, training, and personal relationships of the children exists in Pennsylvania.

11. Petitioner has no information of a custody proceeding concerning the children pending in any court of this Commonwealth or any other State.

12. Petitioner does not know of a person not a party to this proceeding who has physical custody of the children or claims to have custody or visitation rights with respect to the children.

13. The best interests and permanent welfare of the children will be served by granting the relief requested herein because of the attachment of the children to their mother/father and/or the special needs of (child).

14. This matter has not been heard by a custody counselor in the past.

15. Each parent whose physical rights to the children has not been terminated and the persons who have physical custody of the children have been named as parties to this action. All of the persons known to have a claim of right to custody or visitation of the children will be given notice of the pendency of this action and the right to intervene.

16. Petitioner has been advised of the requirement to attend the seminar entitled "Children Coping With Divorce."

WHEREFORE, petitioner respectfully requests this Court to grant:

1. Temporary Emergency Custody to Petitioner;

2. Order that the children be retained by or returned immediately to:

    Pennsylvania / mother / father.

3. Custody and primary residency of the children to the petitioner.

Respectfully submitted,

_____
NAME

IN THE COURT OF COMMON PLEAS

OF _____ COUNTY, PENNSYLVANIA

	:	CIVIL DIVISION
	:	
Plaintiff	:	No.
	:	
vs.	:	
	:	
Defendant	:	

VERIFICATION

I, _____, depose and say that the facts set forth in the foregoing document are true and correct to the best of my knowledge, information, and belief. This is made subject to the penalties of the 18 Pa. C.S.A. Section 4904 relating to unsworn falsification to authorities.

_____

Date: _____

IN THE COURT OF COMMON PLEAS

OF _____ COUNTY, PENNSYLVANIA

	:	CIVIL DIVISION
	:	
Plaintiff	:	No.
	:	
vs.	:	
	:	
Defendant	:	

ORDER OF COURT

AND NOW, this the _____ day of _____, 200____, it is hereby DECREED and ORDERED that the Plaintiff, _____, is AWARDED TEMPORARY CUSTODY of parties _____ minor children

_____

and it is further ORDERED that the Children be immediately returned to the CUSTODY AND CONTROL of Plaintiff pending the proceedings scheduled before the Custody _____ and further Order of this Court.

By the Court:

_____

JUDGE

```
_____      ( IN THE COURT OF COMMON PLEAS OF

            PLAINTIFF,                  (

                                        ( _____COUNTY, PENNSYLVANIA

        v.                              (

                                        ( CIVIL DIVISION

                                        (

_____      ( NO:

            DEFENDANT.
```

AFFIDAVIT OF CONSENT

1.   A complaint in Divorce under Section 3301 (c) of the Divorce Code was filed on (date:) ____/____/____.

2.   The marriage of the Plaintiff and Defendant is irretrievably broken and ninety days have elapsed from the date of filing and Complaint.

3   I consent to the entry of a final decree of Divorce after service of notice of intention to request entry of the decree.

WAIVER OF NOTICE OF INTENTION TO REQUEST
ENTRY OF A DIVORCE DECREE UNDER
SECTION 3301 (c) OF THE DIVORCE CODE

1.   I consent to the entry of a final decree of Divorce without notice.

2.   I understand that I may lose rights concerning alimony, division of property, lawyer's fees, or expenses if I do not claim them before a Divorce is granted.

3.   I understand that I will not be divorced until a Divorce decree is entered by the Court and that a copy of the decree will be sent to me immediately after it is filed with the prothonotary.

I verify that the statements made in this affidavit are true and correct. I understand that false statements herein are made subject to the penalties of 18 Pa C.S. Section 4904 relating to unsworn falsification to authorities.

Date: _____ /_____/_____   _____

                                Plaintiff

```
_____     ( IN THE COURT OF COMMON PLEAS OF
                  PLAINTIFF,         (
                                     (_____COUNTY, PENNSYLVANIA
         v.                          (
                                     ( CIVIL DIVISION
                                     (
_____     ( NO:
                  DEFENDANT.
```

AFFIDAVIT OF CONSENT

1.   A complaint in Divorce under Section 3301 (c) of the Divorce Code was filed on (date:) ____/____/____.

2.   The marriage of the Plaintiff and Defendant is irretrievably broken and ninety days have elapsed from the date of filing and Complaint.

3   I consent to the entry of a final decree of Divorce after service of notice of intention to request entry of the decree.

WAIVER OF NOTICE OF INTENTION TO REQUEST
ENTRY OF A DIVORCE DECREE UNDER
SECTION 3301 (c) OF THE DIVORCE CODE

1.   I consent to the entry of a final decree of Divorce without notice.

2.   I understand that I may lose rights concerning alimony, division of property, lawyer's fees, or expenses if I do not claim them before a Divorce is granted.

3.   I understand that I will not be divorced until a Divorce decree is entered by the Court and that a copy of the decree will be sent to me immediately after it is filed with the prothonotary.

I verify that the statements made in this affidavit are true and correct. I understand that false statements herein are made subject to the penalties of 18 Pa C.S. Section 4904 relating to unsworn falsification to authorities.

Date: _____ /_____/_____   _____
                                  Defendant

_____   (IN THE COURT OF COMMON PLEAS OF

        PLAINTIFF,   (

                    (_____COUNTY, PENNSYLVANIA

     v.   (

                    (CIVIL DIVISION

                    (

_____   (NO:

        DEFENDANT.

DECREE OF DIVORCE

AND NOW, this _____ day of _____, 200_____ (DATE), it is hereby

ORDERED, ADJUDGED, and DECREED, that _____

and _____ are divorced from the bonds of matrimony, and

that Marital Property issues have been previously settled.

                                _____

                              J.

IN THE COURT OF COMMON PLEAS OF _____ COUNTY, PENNSYLVANIA

_____,
   Plaintiff,

         Case No. _____

V.

         Division; _____

_____,
   Defendant

NOTICE OF HEARING

TO: spouse name and address

  Please be advised that a Hearing on the following matter:_____ has been scheduled on the _____ day of _____, 20___, in Courtroom _____ of the _____ County Courthouse, (insert address of Courthouse) before the Honorable _____.

_____
(Insert Plaintiff's Name)

H106 157 REV 8-80

COMMONWEALTH OF PENNSYLVANIA

DEPARTMENT OF HEALTH

VITAL RECORDS

RECORD OF
DIVORCE OR **ANNULMENT**

(CHECK ONE) ☐ ☐

COUNTY

STATE FILE NUMBER

STATE FILE DATE

HUSBAND

1. NAME (First) (Middle) (Last)	2. DATE OF BIRTH (Month) (Day) Year

3. RESIDENCE Street or R.D. City, Boro. or Twp. County State	4. PLACE OF BIRTH (State or Foreign Country)

5. NUMBER OF THIS MARRIAGE	6. RACE WHITE ☐ BLACK ☐ OTHER (Specify) ☐	7. USUAL OCCUPATION

WIFE

8. MAIDEN NAME (First) (Middle) (Last)	9. DATE OF BIRTH (Month) (Day) Year

10. RESIDENCE Street or R.D. City, Boro. or Twp. County State	11. PLACE OF BIRTH (State or Foreign Country)

12. NUMBER OF THIS MARRIAGE	6. RACE WHITE ☐ BLACK ☐ OTHER (Specify) ☐	14. USUAL OCCUPATION

15. PLACE OF THIS MARRIAGE (County) (State or Foreign Country)	16. DATE OF THIS MARRIAGE (Month) (Day) (year)

17A. NUMBER OF CHILDREN THIS MARRIAGE	17B. NUMBER OF DEPENDENT CHILDREN UNDER 18	18. PLAINTIFF HUSBAND ☐ WIFE ☐ OTHER (Specify) ☐	19. DECREE GRANTED TO HUSBAND ☐ WIFE ☐ OTHER (Specify) ☐

20. NUMBER OF CHILDREN TO CUSTODY OF	HUSBAND ☐ WIFE ☐ SPLIT CUSTODY ☐ OTHER (Specify)	21. LEGAL GROUNDS FOR DIVORCE OR ANNULMENT

22. DATE OF DECREE (Month) (Day) (Year)	23. DATE REPORT SENT TO VITAL RECORDS (Month) (Day) (Year)

24. SIGNATURE OF TRANSCRIBING CLERK

(IN THE COURT OF COMMON PLEAS OF

_____
                    PLAINTIFF,   (

            (_____COUNTY, PENNSYLVANIA

       v.   (

            (CIVIL DIVISION

            (

_____   (NO:
                    DEFENDANT.

NOTICE OF INTENTION TO REQUEST
ENTRY OF DIVORCE DECREE

TO: _____
      Plaintiff/Defendant

You have been sued in an action for divorce. You have failed to answer the Complaint or file a counteraffidavit to plaintiff's affidavit. Therefore, on or after _____, 200___, the plaintiff can request the Court to enter a final decree in divorce.

If you do not file with the Prothonotary of the Court an answer with your signature notarized or verified or a counteraffidavit by the above date, the Court can enter a final decree in divorce. Unless you have already filed with the Court a written claim for economic relief, you must do so by the above date or the Court may grant the divorce and you will lose forever the right to ask for economic relief. A COUNTERAFFIDAVIT WHICH YOU MAY FILE WITH THE PROTHONOTARY OF THE COURT IS ATTACHED TO THIS NOTICE.

_____
Plaintiff/Defendant

_____   (IN THE COURT OF COMMON PLEAS OF

PLAINTIFF,   (

    (_____COUNTY, PENNSYLVANIA

v.   (

    (CIVIL DIVISION

    (

_____   (NO:

DEFENDANT.

COUNTERAFFIDAVIT UNDER § 3301(d) OF
THE DIVORCE CODE

1.   Check either (a) or (b):

    (a)   I do not oppose the entry of a divorce decree   [   ]

    (b)   I oppose the entry of a divorce decree because
        [Check (i), (ii), or both]

        (i)   The parties to this action have not lived separate and apart
            for a period of at least two (thee) years.   [   ]

        (ii)   The marriage is not irretrievably broken.   [   ]

2.   Check either (a) or (b):

    (a)   I do not wish to make any claims for economic relief. I understand that I may lose rights concerning alimony, division of property, lawyer's fees or expenses if I do not claim them before a divorce is granted.   [   ]

    (b)   I wish to claim economic relief which may include alimony, division of property, lawyer's fees or expenses or other important rights.   [   ]

    I verify that the statements made in this counteraffidavit are true and correct. I understand that false statements are made subject to the penalties of 18 Pa. C.S. § 4904 relating to unsworn falsification to authorities.

_____
                [Name]

Date: _____

NOTICE: If you do not wish to oppose the entry of a divorce decree and you do not wish to make any claim for economic relief, you need not file this counteraffidavit.

NOTICE TO FILE SOCIAL SECURITY NUMBERS

PURSUANT TO THE 23 P.S. SECTION 4304.1(a)(3) PARTIES TO A DIVORCE ARE REQUIRED TO PROVIDE THEIR SOCIAL SECURITY NUMBERS TO THE COURT. PLEASE SUBMIT THE SOCIAL SECURITY NUMBERS OF THE PARTIES TO YOUR DIVORCE TO THE PROTHONOTARY.

PLEASE FILL IN THE APPROPRIATE INFORMATION AND RETURN TO THE PROTHONOTARY OFFICE—THESE INFORMATION SHEETS WILL BE KEPT IN A SEPARATE FILE.

DATE: _____

DOCKET NUMBER: _____

PLAINTIFF/PETITIONER SS#: _____

NAME: _____

DEFENDANT/RESPONDENT SS#: _____

NAME: _____

Office of Clerk of Records
Prothonotary Division
County Courthouse

_____   (IN THE COURT OF COMMON PLEAS OF

PLAINTIFF,   (

(_____COUNTY, PENNSYLVANIA

v.   (

(CIVIL DIVISION

(

_____   (NO:

DEFENDANT.

NOTICE OF INTENTION TO RETAKE PRIOR NAME

Notice is hereby given that the Plaintiff/Defendant in the above matter, having been granted a Final Decree in Divorce, on the _____ day of _____, 200___, hereby elects to retake and hereafter use her previous name of _____ _____, and gives this written notice avowing her intention in accordance with the provisions of 54 Pa. C.S.A. § 704.

_____
Signature

TO BE KNOWN AS:

_____

On the _____ day of _____, 200____, before me, a Notary Public, personally appeared _____, known to me to be the person whose name is subscribed to the within document and acknowledged that he/she executed the foregoing for the purpose therein contained.

IN WITNESS THEREOF, I have hereunto set my hand and seal.

_____
Notary Public

This page intentionally left blank.

Domestic Relations Information Sheet

DATE	CASE I.D. NO.

INFORMATION ON PARENTS

FATHER OF CHILDREN *(First Name)* *(Middle Initial)* *(Last Name)*	ALIAS, IF ANY

MAILING ADDRESS	RESIDENTIAL ADDRESS, IF DIFFERENT FROM MAILING ADDRESS

DATE OF BIRTH	SOCIAL SECURITY NO	DPW NO

HEIGHT	WEIGHT	RACE	HAIR	EYES	DISTINGUISHING FEATURES

PLACE OF EMPLOYMENT	MEDICAL INSURANCE CARRIER NAME, ADDRESS

HOME PHONE NO.	WORK PHONE NO.	POLICY NO.	CHILDREN COVERED? ☐ Yes ☐ No

OCCUPATION	ATTORNEY'S NAME AND ADDRESS

SALARY $_____ per _____	ATTORNEY I.D. NO.

MOTHER OF CHILDREN *(First Name)* *(Middle Initial)* *(Last Name)*	ALIAS, IF ANY

MAILING ADDRESS	RESIDENTIAL ADDRESS, IF DIFFERENT FROM MAILING ADDRESS

DATE OF BIRTH	SOCIAL SECURITY NO	DPW NO

HEIGHT	WEIGHT	RACE	HAIR	EYES	DISTINGUISHING FEATURES

PLACE OF EMPLOYMENT	MEDICAL INSURANCE CARRIER NAME, ADDRESS

HOME PHONE NO.	WORK PHONE NO.	POLICY NO.	CHILDREN COVERED? ☐ Yes ☐ No

OCCUPATION	ATTORNEY'S NAME AND ADDRESS

SALARY $_____ per _____	ATTORNEY I.D. NO.

RECEIVING ASSISTANCE? ☐ Yes ☐ No	DPW NO.	DISTRICT RECEIVING FROM	SEMI-MONTHLY GRANT AMOUNT	TOTAL NO. OF PEOPLE IN HOUSEHOLD

PARTIES EVER MARRIED? ☐ Yes ☐ No	MARRIAGE DATE	PLACE	DATE OF SEPARATION	DATE OF DIVORCE	PLACE

MATERNAL GRANDMOTHER'S MAIDEN NAME	MATERNAL GRANDFATHER'S NAME

09-788

INFORMATION ON CARETAKER OF CHILD(REN) OTHER THAN PARENTS (IF ANY)

NAME	(First)	(Middle Initial)	(Last)	RELATIONSHIP	DATE OF BIRTH

ADDRESS		HOME PHONE NO.	WORK PHONE NO.
		SOCIAL SECURITY NO.	

INFORMATION ON CHILDREN

NAME (First) (Middle Initial) (Last)	SEX	DATE OF BIRTH
	☐ Male ☐ Female	

SOCIAL SECURITY NO.	PLACE OF BIRTH	ACTIVE ON CASH ASSISTANCE?
		☐ Yes ☐ No

FATHER LISTED ON BIRTH CERTIFICATE?	BORN OUT OF WEDLOCK?	WAS PATERNITY ESTABLISHED?	DATE OF PATERNITY ESTABLISHMENT
☐ Yes ☐ No	☐ Yes ☐ No	☐ Yes ☐ No	

NAME (First) (Middle Initial) (Last)	SEX	DATE OF BIRTH
	☐ Male ☐ Female	

SOCIAL SECURITY NO.	PLACE OF BIRTH	ACTIVE ON CASH ASSISTANCE?
		☐ Yes ☐ No

FATHER LISTED ON BIRTH CERTIFICATE?	BORN OUT OF WEDLOCK?	WAS PATERNITY ESTABLISHED?	DATE OF PATERNITY ESTABLISHMENT
☐ Yes ☐ No	☐ Yes ☐ No	☐ Yes ☐ No	

NAME (First) (Middle Initial) (Last)	SEX	DATE OF BIRTH
	☐ Male ☐ Female	

SOCIAL SECURITY NO.	PLACE OF BIRTH	ACTIVE ON CASH ASSISTANCE?
		☐ Yes ☐ No

FATHER LISTED ON BIRTH CERTIFICATE?	BORN OUT OF WEDLOCK?	WAS PATERNITY ESTABLISHED?	DATE OF PATERNITY ESTABLISHMENT
☐ Yes ☐ No	☐ Yes ☐ No	☐ Yes ☐ No	

NAME (First) (Middle Initial) (Last)	SEX	DATE OF BIRTH
	☐ Male ☐ Female	

SOCIAL SECURITY NO.	PLACE OF BIRTH	ACTIVE ON CASH ASSISTANCE?
		☐ Yes ☐ No

FATHER LISTED ON BIRTH CERTIFICATE?	BORN OUT OF WEDLOCK?	WAS PATERNITY ESTABLISHED?	DATE OF PATERNITY ESTABLISHMENT
☐ Yes ☐ No	☐ Yes ☐ No	☐ Yes ☐ No	

NAME (First) (Middle Initial) (Last)	SEX	DATE OF BIRTH
	☐ Male ☐ Female	

SOCIAL SECURITY NO.	PLACE OF BIRTH	ACTIVE ON CASH ASSISTANCE?
		☐ Yes ☐ No

FATHER LISTED ON BIRTH CERTIFICATE?	BORN OUT OF WEDLOCK?	WAS PATERNITY ESTABLISHED?	DATE OF PATERNITY ESTABLISHMENT
☐ Yes ☐ No	☐ Yes ☐ No	☐ Yes ☐ No	

09-788 (Reverse)

_____

Plaintiff(s)

COURT OF COMMON PLEAS
FAMILY DIVISION

TERM.

vs.

Defendant(s)

No.

NOTICE TO DEFEND AND CLAIM RIGHTS

You have been sued in court for

☐ Divorce   ☐ Annulment of Marriage
☐ Support   ☐ Custody and Visitation
☐ Division of Property   ☐ Alimony
☐ Temporary Alimony   ☐ Attorney Fees
☐ Costs

You have been sued in court. If you wish to defend against the claims set forth in the following pages, you must take prompt action. You are warned that if you fail to do so, the case may proceed without you and a decree of divorce or annulment may be entered against you by the court. A judgment may also be entered against you for any other claim of relief requested in these papers by the plaintiff. You may lose money or property or other rights important to you, including custody or visitation of your children.

When the ground for the divorce is indignities or irretrievable breakdown of the marriage, you may request marriage counseling. A list of marriage counselors is available in the Office of the Prothonotary at Room 286 City Hall, Philadelphia, PA 19107.

IF YOU DO NOT FILE A CLAIM FOR ALIMONY, DIVISION OF PROPERTY, LAWYER'S FEES OR EXPENSES BEFORE A DIVORCE OR ANNULMENT IS GRANTED, YOU MAY LOSE THE RIGHT TO CLAIM ANY OF THEM.
YOU SHOULD TAKE THIS PAPER TO YOUR LAWYER AT ONCE. IF YOU DO NOT HAVE A LAWYER OR CANNOT AFFORD ONE, GO TO OR TELEPHONE THE OFFICE SET FORTH BELOW TO FIND OUT WHERE YOU CAN GET LEGAL HELP.
Lawyer Reference Service
    One Reading Center
Philadelphia, Pennsylvania   19107
      Telephone: 238-1701

ADVERTENCIA SOBRE COMO DEFENDERSE Y RECLAMAR DERECHOS

You have been sued in court for

☐ Divorcio   ☐ Annulacion de Matrimonia
☐ Pension Alimenticia   ☐ Custodia y Visitacion
  (Mantenimiento)
☐ Division de Propiedad   ☐ Pension Alimenticia
☐ Pension Alimenticia   ☐ Costas de Abogado
  Temporana   ☐ Costas

Usted ha sido demandado en corte. Si usted desea defender el reclamo puesto en contra suya en las siguientes paginas, tiene que tomar accion inmediatamente. Se le advierta que si falla en hacerlo, el casa puede ser procasado sin su de usted por la corte. Un juicio tambien puede ser registrado en contra de usted por la corte. Un jucio tambien puede ser registrado en su contra por cualquier otro reclamo o peticion requerida en ostos papeles por el querellante. Usted puede perder dinero, propiedad o otros derechos importantes para usted, incluyendo custodia o visitacion para sus ninos.

Cuando la causa del divorcio es maltrato o trastorno irrearable en el matrimonio, usted debe solicitar consejeria matrimonial. Una lista de consejeros matrimoniales esta disponible en las oficinas del pro-thonotario en Cuarto 286 de la Alcadia, Filadelfia, PA 19107 (Room 286 City Hall, Philadelphia, PA 19107.

SI USTED NO REGISTRA UN RECLAMADO PARA LA PENCION ALIMENTICIA, LA REPARTICION DE PROPIEDADES, EL HONORARIO DEL ABOGADO O GASTOS ANTES DE QUE EL UN DIVORCIO O ANNULACION SEA OTORGADO, USTED PUEDE PERDER EL DERECHO DE RECLAMAR CULAQUIERA DE ESTOS.
USTED DEBE LLEVAR ESTE PAPEL A SU ABOGADO INMEDIAMENTE. SI USTED NO TIENE UN ABOGADO O NO PUEDE PAGAR POR LOS SERVICIOS DE UNO, VAYA O LLAME A LA OFICINA INDICADA, PARA AVERIGUAR DONDE PUEDE OBTENER ASISTENCIA LEGAL.
SERVICIO DE REFERENCIA DE ABOGADO
    Uno Reading Centro
  Filadelfia, Pennsylvania   19107
      Telefono: 238-1701

_____

Former Domestic Relations Proceeding   ☐ *Yes*   ☐ *No*
If child support is claimed, is such child
or children receiving Public Assistance   ☐ *Yes*   ☐ *No*

Domestic Relations No.

Complaint In Divorce

<u>COUNT I - Divorce</u>

Plaintiff, by (his/her) attorney(s)   , respectfully represents:

1. Plaintiff is   , who currently resides at
(Name)   (Address)
in the City of   , County of   , Pennsylvania, since
(Date)

2. Defendant is   , who currently resides at
(Name)   (Address)
in the City of   , County of   , Pennsylvania, since

3. Plaintiff and defendant are sui juris, and both have been bona fide residents of the Commonwealth of Pennsylvania for a period of more than six (6) months immediately preceding the filing of this Complaint. (If only one is a resident of the Commonwealth of Pennsylvania for the required time, so state.)

4. The parties were married on the   day of   ,   , at
State of   A certified copy (the original) of the marriage certificate is attached hereto, made a part hereof and marked Exhibit "A." (Explanation if unavailable)

5. (State cause of action and section(s) of Divorce Code under which plaintiff is proceeding.)

6. There have been no prior actions of divorce or for annulment between the parties except

7. The parties have/have not entered into a written agreement as to (support, visitation of children, alimony, and property division.) (A true and correct copy of said agreement is attached hereto, made a part hereof and marked Exhibit "B.")

WHEREFORE, plaintiff requests your Honorable Court to enter a decree in divorce, divorcing plaintiff and defendant. (In the event it is desired that the agreement be made part of the Court Order, add: "and the agreement attached hereto as Exhibit "B" be incorporated in the decree and entered as an order of this Court.")

<u>COUNT II - Equitable Distribution</u>

8. Paragraphs 1 through 4 of this Complaint are incorporated herein by reference as though set forth in full .

9. Plaintiff and defendant have acquired property, both real and personal during their marriage from
until   , the date of their separation.

10. Plaintiff and defendant have been unable to agree as to an equitable division of said property.

WHEREFORE, plaintiff requests your Honorable Court to equitably divide all marital property.

<u>COUNT III - Alimony</u>

11. Paragraphs 1 through 4 of this Complaint are incorporated herein by reference as though set forth in full.

12. Plaintiff lacks sufficient property to provide for (his/her) reasonable means and is unable to support (himself/herself)   through appropriate employment.

13. Plaintiff requires reasonable support to adequately maintain (himself/herself) in accordance with the standard of living established during the marriage.

WHEREFORE, plaintiff requests your Honorable Court to enter an award of alimony.

PAGE 2 of 4

COUNT IV - Support for Children

14. Paragraphs 1 through 4 of this Complaint are incorporated herein by reference as though set forth in full .

15. Plaintiff and defendant are parents of   unemancipated children:

Name(s)   Age   Sex   Date of Birth   Residence

16. Support is sought for (Names of children)

17. Plaintiff is (is not) on Public Assistance and receives $ per   for wife and/or children.

18. Defendant earns in excess of $ (net/gross) per year and has assets in excess of $

19. Defendant has failed to provide for adequate and reasonable support for said children in accordance with the standard of living of the parties.   or   (Defendant has been paying $ per   for support of said children and plaintiff desires said payments be continued by Order of the Court.

WHEREFORE, plaintiff requests an award of reasonable and adequate support for the children of the parties.

COUNT V - Alimony Pendente Lite, Counsel Fees, Costs and Expenses

20. Paragraphs 1 through 4 and 18 of this Complaint are incorporated herein by reference as though set forth in full .

21. Plaintiff has employed counsel, but is unable to pay the necessary and reasonable attorney's fees for said counsel.

22. Plaintiff is unable to sustain herself/himself during the course of this litigation.

WHEREFORE, plaintiff requests your Honorable Court to enter an award of Alimony Pendente lite, interim counsel fees, costs and expenses, until final hearing and thereupon award such additional counsel fees, costs and expenses as deemed appropriate.

COUNT VI - Custody
Partial Custody and/or Visitation

23. Paragraphs 1 through 4 and 15 of this Complaint are incorporated herein by reference as though set forth in full .

24. In the past five years, the parties' children have resided (addresses where the children have resided and the name and present address of the parties with whom they have resided.)

25. Plaintiff has/has not participated (as a party, witness, or in any other capacity) in any other litigation concerning the custody of the same child/children in this or any other State. (Note: if this averment is in the affirmative, plaintiff shall explain such participation and the status or disposition of such case.)

26. Plaintiff has/has no information of any custody proceeding concerning the child/children pending in this or any other case. (Note: if this averment is in the affirmative, plaintiff shall supply all available information concerning such proceeding.)

27. Plaintiff knows/does not know of any person not a party to the proceedings who has physical custody of the child/children or who claims to have custody or visitation rights with respect to the child/children. (Note: If this averment is in the affirmative, plaintiff shall supply all available information concerning such person/persons.)

28. The best interest of the child(ren) would be served by granting requested relief.

WHEREFORE, plaintiff prays your Honorable Court to grant custody   partial custody   visitation right to plaintiff.

BY: _____

Attorneys for Plaintiff

VERIFICATION TO COMPLAINT IN DIVORCE

Plaintiff verifies that the statements made in this complaint are true and correct. Plaintiff understands that false statements herein are made subject to the penalties of 18 Pa. C.S. Section 4904, relating to unsworn falsification to authorities.

_____

PLAINTIFF

_____

ATTORNEY FOR PLAINTIFF

_____

DATE

COMMONWEALTH OF PENNSYLVANIA
COUNTY OF PHILADELPHIA

COUNSELING NOTICE UNDER PA. R.C.P. RULE 1920.45(a) (1)

COURT OF COMMON PLEAS
Family Court Division

vs. _____ Term, 20_____

No. _____

COUNSELING NOTICE

The Divorce Code of Pennsylvania requires that you be notified of the availability of counseling where a divorce is sought under any of the following grounds:

| Section | 3301(a) | (6) | Indignities |

Section   3301(c)   Irretrievable Breakdown
                          Mutual Consent

Section   3301(d)   Irretrievable Breakdown
                          Two (2) Year Separation Where
                            the Court Determines That
                            There is a Reasonable Pros-
                            pect of Reconciliation

A list of qualified professionals is available for inspection in the office of the Appointments Clerk of Family Court in B-16   or in the office of the Chief of the Domestic Relations Branch of the Family Court of Philadelphia, 34 S. 11th Street.

_____
Counsel for

5-174

COURT OF COMMON PLEAS

FAMILY COURT DIVISION

_____, 20_____

V.

NO._____

NOTICE TO THE DEFENDANT

If you wish to deny any of the statements set forth in this affidavit, you must file a counter-affidavit within twenty days after this affidavit has been served on you or the statements will be admitted.

**PLAINTIFF'S AFFIDAVIT UNDER SECTION 3301 (d)
OF THE DIVORCE CODE**

1.   A complaint in divorce under Section 3301 (d) of the Divorce Code was filed on

_____.

2.   (a)   The parties to this action separated on _____ and have continued to live separate and apart for a period of at least two years.

    (b)   The marriage is irretrievably broken.

I understand that I may lose rights concerning alimony, division of property, lawyer's fees or expenses if I do not claim them before a divorce is granted.

I verify that the statements made in this affidavit are true and correct. I understand that false statements herein are made subject to the penalties of 18 Pa.C.S. § 4904 relating to unsworn falsification to authorities.

Date:_____   _____

(Plaintiff)

IN THE COURT OF COMMON PLEAS OF PHILADELPHIA COUNTY
FAMILY COURT DIVISION

Plaintiff	:	TERM, 20
	:	NO.
vs.	:	IN DIVORCE
	:	CAUSE:
Defendant	:	

PRAECIPE TO TRANSMIT RECORD

Transmit the record, together with the following information, to the Court for entry of a divorce decree:

1. Ground for divorce: Irretrievable breakdown under Section 3301(c) 3301(d) of the Divorce Code (strike out inapplicable section).
2. Date and manner of service of Complaint:_____
_____
3. Complete either paragraph (a) or (b):
   (a) Date of execution of the Affidavit of Consent required by Section 3301(c) of the Divorce Code:
   by Plaintiff: _____   by Defendant: _____
   (b) (1) Date of execution of Plaintiff's Affidavit required by Section 3301(d) of the Divorce Code: _____
   (2) Date of filing of Plaintiff's Affidavit required by Section 3301(d):_____
   (3) Date of service of Plaintiff's Affidavit upon Defendant: _____
4. Complete the appropriate paragraphs:
   (a) Related claims pending: _____
   _____
   (b) Claims withdrawn: _____
   _____
   (c) Claims settled by agreement of the parties: _____
   _____
   (d) State whether any written agreement is to be incorporated into the Divorce Decree
   _____
   If yes, attach a true and correct copy of the fully executed agreement to the proposed Decree that is submitted herewith.
5. I certify that the Notice of Intent to File Praecipe to Transmit as required by Rule 1920.42(c) or 1920.42*(d) was mailed on _____ and a copy thereof is attached. I further certify that all other documents required by Rule 1920.42*(e) are enclosed herewith.

_____
Attorney for (Plaintiff)
(Defendant)

IN THE COURT OF COMMON PLEAS OF PHILADELPHIA COUNTY
FAMILY DIVISION

<table>
<tr><td></td><td>Plaintiff</td><td>:</td><td></td></tr>
<tr><td></td><td></td><td>:</td><td></td></tr>
<tr><td>vs.</td><td></td><td>:</td><td>_____ TERM</td></tr>
<tr><td></td><td></td><td>:</td><td></td></tr>
<tr><td></td><td></td><td>:</td><td>NO.</td></tr>
<tr><td></td><td>Defendant</td><td>:</td><td></td></tr>
</table>

NOTICE OF INTENT TO FILE PRAECIPE TO TRANSMIT

You are hereby given notice that five days following the mailing of this notice, a Praecipe to Transmit Record, together with a proposed Final Decree in Divorce, will be filed in this matter with the Appointment Clerk's Office, Room B-16, 34 S. 11th Street, Phila., PA 19107. Exact copies of the Praecipe and the proposed Final Decree in Divorce are enclosed herewith.

After the praecipe and proposed Final Decree in Divorce are filed, you will have a period of ten days during which you may file objections to the entry of the Final Decree based upon this Praecipe. If you dispute any of the information on the Praecipe or Final Decree you must act within that ten-day period. Any objections must be filed in writing with the Appointment Clerk's Office, Room B-16, 34 S. 11th Street, Phila., PA 19107. If no objections are filed before the expiration of the ten-day period, this case will be submitted to the Court for entry of the Final Decree.

_____, 20_____   _____
                                                              Plaintiff

IN THE COURT OF COMMON PLEAS OF PHILADELPHIA COUNTY
FAMILY COURT DIVISION

Plaintiff	:	TERM, 20
	:	NO.
vs.	:	IN DIVORCE
	:	CAUSE:
Defendant	:	

WAIVER OF NOTICE OF INTENTION TO REQUEST
ENTRY OF A DIVORCE DECREE UNDER
§ 3301(c) OF THE DIVORCE CODE

1. I consent to the entry of a final decree of divorce without notice.

2. I understand that I may lose rights concerning alimony, division of property, lawyer's fees or expenses if I do not claim them before a divorce is granted.

3. I understand that I will not be divorced until a divorce decree is entered by the Court and that a copy of the decree will be sent to me immediately after it is filed with the prothonotary.

I verify that the statements made in this affidavit are true and correct. I understand that false statements herein are made subject to the penalties of 18 Pa.C.S. §4904 relating to unsworn falsification to authorities.

Date: _____   _____
                                                                            Plaintiff/Defendant

FORM NO. 4

IN THE COURT OF COMMON PLEAS OF PHILADELPHIA COUNTY
FAMILY COURT DIVISION

Plaintiff	:	TERM, 20
	:	NO.
vs.	:	IN DIVORCE
	:	CAUSE:
Defendant	:	

NOTICE OF INTENTION TO REQUEST ENTRY
OF § 3301(c) DIVORCE DECREE

TO:_____
   (PLAINTIFF) (DEFENDANT)

*You have signed a §3301(c) affidavit consenting to the entry of a divorce decree. Therefore, **on or after**   , 20   , the other party can request the Court to enter a final decree in divorce.*

Unless you have already filed with the Court a written claim for economic relief, you must do so be the date in the paragraph above, or the Court may grant the divorce and you will lose forever the right to ask for economic relief. The filing of the form counter-affidavit alone does not protect your economic claims.

YOU SHOULD TAKE THIS PAPER TO YOUR LAWYER AT ONCE. IF YOU DO NOT HAVE A LAWYER OR CANNOT AFFORD ONE, GO TO OR TELEPHONE THE OFFICE SET FORTH BELOW TO FIND OUT WHERE YOU CAN GET LEGAL HELP.

LAWYER REFERRAL AND INFORMATION SERVICE
PHILADELPHIA BAR ASSOCIATION
1101 MARKET STREET, 11TH FLOOR
PHILADELPHIA, PENNSYLVANIA 19107-2911

TELEPHONE: (215) 238-6333

IN THE COURT OF COMMON PLEAS OF PHILADELPHIA COUNTY
FAMILY COURT DIVISION

Plaintiff	:	TERM, 20
	:	NO.
vs.	:	IN DIVORCE
	:	CAUSE:
Defendant	:	

COUNTER-AFFIDAVIT UNDER
§ 3301(c) OF THE DIVORCE CODE

I wish to claim economic relief which may include alimony, division of property, lawyer's fees or expenses or other important rights.

I understand that I must file my economic claims with the Clerk of the Family Court in writing and serve them on the other party. If I fail to do so before the date set forth on the Notice of Intention to Request Divorce Decree, the divorce decree may be entered without further notice to me, and I shall be unable thereafter to file any economic claims.

I verify that the statements made in this counter-affidavit are true and correct. I understand that false statements herein are made subject to the penalties of 18 Pa. C.S. § 4904, relating to unsworn falsification to authorities.

_____   Date:_____
(PLAINTIFF) (DEFENDANT)

NOTICE: IF YOU DO NOT WISH TO CLAIM ECONOMIC RELIEF, YOU SHOULD NOT FILE THIS COUNTER-AFFIDAVIT.

IN THE COURT OF COMMON PLEAS OF PHILADELPHIA COUNTY
FAMILY DIVISION

```
                               :
        Plaintiff

vs.                            :        NO.

        Defendant             :        IN DIVORCE
```

<u>NOTICE OF INTENTION TO REQUEST ENTRY OF DIVORCE DECREE</u>
(CASES UNDER SECTION 3301(c) OF THE DIVORCE CODE)

TO: _____
       (PLAINTIFF/DEFENDANT)

You are hereby given notice that twenty (20) days following the mailing of this Notice, which will be on or after _____, 20___, a Praecipe to Transmit Record will be filed in this matter, requesting that a Final Decree in Divorce be entered. Said Praecipe will be filed with the Clerk of the Family Court, Room B-16, 34 South 11th Street, Philadelphia, PA 19107.

Exact copies of the Praecipe and the proposed Final Decree are also attached hereto.

_____   _____
(Date of Mailing)   Counsel for Plaintiff/Defendant

```
_____,          : IN THE COURT OF COMMON PLEAS
              Petitioner    :
              v.            : OF PHILADELPHIA COUNTY, PENNSYLVANIA
                            :
                            : DOCKET NO.
                            :
_____,          :
              Respondent    :
```

MARITAL PROPERTY SETTLEMENT AGREEMENT

1.   A Complaint in Divorce under Section 3301(c) of the Divorce Code was filed on _____ (date).

2.   The marriage of plaintiff and defendant is irretrievably broken and ninety (90) days have elapsed from the date of filing and service of the Complaint
_____ (Name and Address)
hereinafter referred to herein as Wife/Husband, *[Note: Strike out inapplicable designation, i.e. Wife or Husband throughout]*

and
_____ (Name and Address)
hereinafter referred to as Wife/Husband, agree:

The parties were lawfully married on _____, 20 _____ at _____
_____. (Name and Location)

3.   The parties nevertheless desire to resolve certain issues and consequently, have entered into this agreement.

The parties have child(ren) born of this marriage,

1)._____
Name   Age   Date of Birth

2)._____
Name   Age   Date of Birth

3)._____
Name   Age   Date of Birth

The parties have mad a complete disclosure to one another of financial matters and each is satisfied that they have had sufficient disclosure of the parties individual and joint finances.

The Wife/Husband shall assume the following debts and shall not hold the Wife/Husband responsible for the same:

_____
_____
_____

The Wife/Husband shall assume the following debts and shall not hold the Wife/Husband responsible for the same:

_____
_____
_____

Neither party shall incur any further debts which may result in joint liability. In the event that either party incurs a debt on joint credit of the parties, that party shall be responsible for the total amount of that debt.

Personal property of the parties shall be divided as follows:
The Wife/Husband shall have the following property:

_____
_____
_____

The Wife/Husband shall have the following property:

_____
_____
_____

All personal property has been satisfactorily divided to the agreement of both parties. If any debts are associated with the items of property previously divided or divided herein, the party receiving the same shall assume the debt and hold the other party harmless from such debts.

The Wife/Husband shall have possession of the residence owned by the parties located at _____. Expenses related to the residence shall be borne by the parties as follows: Wife/Husband to refinance the marital residence to remove Wife/Husband's name from all Mortgages, Promissory Notes, and/or other related obligations or debts associated with the marital residence. Any cost to refinance the marital residence shall be borne by the Wife/Husband.

The parties agree that this agreement is intended to be a final disposition of the matters agreed upon herein. This agreement may be introduced into evidence and incorporated in a final decree of dissolution of marriage. In the event that any disputes occur regarding this agreement, the prevailing party shall be entitled to reasonable attorney's fees regarding such enforcement.

This Is A Legally Enforceable Agreement. Read Carefully And Obtain Legal Counseling before Executing This Agreement.

_____   _____
Signature of Wife/Husband   Date

_____   _____
Signature of Wife/Husband   Date

_____   _____
Witness for Wife/Husband   Date

_____   _____
Witness for Wife/Husband   Date

IN THE COURT OF COMMON PLEAS OF PHILADELPHIA COUNTY FAMILY COURT DIVISION

Plaintiff	:	TERM, 20
	:	NO.
vs.	:	IN DIVORCE
	:	CAUSE:
Defendant	:	

NOTICE OF INTENTION TO REQUEST ENTRY OF § 3301(d) DIVORCE DECREE

TO:_____
(PLAINTIFF) (DEFENDANT)

You have been sued in an action for divorce. You have failed to answer the complaint or file a counter-affidavit to the §3301(d) affidavit. Therefore, on or after _____, 20___, the other party can request the court to enter a final decree in divorce.

If you do not file with the Clerk of the Family Court an answer with your signature notarized or verified or a counter-affidavit by the above date, the court can enter a final decree in divorce. A counter-affidavit which you may file with the Clerk of the Family Court is attached to this notice.

Unless you have already filed with the court a written claim for economic relief, you must do so by the above date or the court may grant the divorce and you will lose forever the right to ask for economic relief. The filing of the form counter-affidavit alone does not protect your economic claims.

YOU SHOULD TAKE THIS PAPER TO YOUR LAWYER AT ONCE. IF YOU DO NOT HAVE A LAWYER OR CANNOT AFFORD ONE, GO TO OR TELEPHONE THE OFFICE SET FORTH BELOW TO FIND OUT WHERE YOU CAN GET LEGAL HELP.

**LAWYER REFERRAL AND INFORMATION SERVICE
PHILADELPHIA BAR ASSOCIATION
1101 MARKET STREET, 11TH FLOOR
PHILADELPHIA, PENNSYLVANIA 19107-2911**

TELEPHONE: (215) 238-6333

IN THE COURT OF COMMON PLEAS OF PHILADELPHIA COUNTY
FAMILY COURT DIVISION

	:	TERM, 20
vs.	:	NO.
	:	IN DIVORCE
	:	CAUSE: IRRETRIEVABLE BREAKDOWN
		SECTION 3301(d)

COUNTER-AFFIDAVIT UNDER SECTION 3301(D) OF THE DIVORCE CODE

1. Check either (a) or (b):
(a) I do not oppose the entry of a divorce decree.

(b) I oppose the entry of a divorce decree because

(Check (i), (ii) or both):

(i) The parties to this action have not lived separate and apart for a period of at least two years.

(ii) The marriage is not irretrievably broken.

2. Check either (a) or (b):

(a) I do not wish to make any claims for economic relief. I understand that I may lose rights concerning alimony, division of property, lawyer's fees or expenses if I do not claim them before a divorce is granted.

(b) I wish to claim economic relief which my include alimony, division of property, lawyer's fees or expenses or other important rights.

I verify that the statements made in this counteraffidavit are true and correct. I understand that false statements herein are made subject to the penalties of 18 Pa.C.S. §4904 relating to unsworn falsification to authorities.

Date: _____   _____
                                     Plaintiff/Defendant

NOTICE: If you do not wish to oppose the entry of a divorce decree and you do not wish to make any claim for economic relief, you need not file this counteraffidavit.

IN THE COURT OF COMMON PLEAS OF PHILADELPHIA COUNTY
FAMILY COURT DIVISION

	:	TERM, 20
	:	NO.
vs.	:	IN DIVORCE
	:	CAUSE: IRRETRIEVABLE BREAKDOWN SECTION 3301(d)
	:	

NOTICE OF INTENTION TO REQUEST ENTRY OF DIVORCE DECREE
(CASES UNDER SECTION 3301(c) OF THE DIVORCE CODE)

TO: _____
     Counsel for Plaintiff/Defendant

     Plaintiff/Defendant intends to file with the Court the attached Praecipe to Transmit Record on or after _____, 20___, requesting that a Final Decree in Divorce be entered. A copy of the proposed Final Decree is also attached hereto.

_____   _____
(Date of Mailing)   Counsel for Plaintiff/Defendant

Affidavit Alleging Requisite Separation Period for a Unilateral No-Fault Divorce

IN THE COURT OF COMMON PLEAS
OF _____ COUNTY PENNSYLVANIA

_____,   No.

Plaintiff

_____,

Defendant

NOTICE TO THE PLAINTIFF

If you wish to deny any of the statements set forth in this affidavit, you must file a counteraffidavit within twenty days after this affidavit has been served on you or the statements will be admitted.

DEFENDANT'S AFFIDAVIT UNDER
SECTION 3301 (d) of the DIVORCE CODE

1.   The parties to this action separated on _____ and have continued to live separate and apart for a period of at least the time period specified in Section 3301 (d) of the Divorce Code.

2.   The marriage is irretrievably broken.

3.   I understand that I may lose rights concerning alimony, division of property, lawyer's fees, or expenses if I do not claim them before a Divorce is granted.

I verify that the statements made in this affidavit are true and correct. I understand that false statements herein are made subject to the penalties of 18 Pa.C.S. Section 4904 relating to unsworn falsification to authorities.

Date:_____   _____

Defendant

INDEX

SPHINX® PUBLISHING'S NATIONAL TITLES

Valid in All 50 States

LEGAL SURVIVAL IN BUSINESS

The Complete Book of Corporate Forms	$24.95
How to Form a Delaware Corporation from Any State	$24.95
How to Form a Limited Liability Company	$22.95
Incorporate in Nevada from Any State	$24.95
How to Form a Nonprofit Corporation	$24.95
How to Form Your Own Corporation (3E)	$24.95
How to Form Your Own Partnership	$22.95
How to Register Your Own Copyright (4E)	$24.95
How to Register Your Own Trademark (3E)	$21.95
Most Valuable Business Legal Forms You'll Ever Need (3E)	$21.95

LEGAL SURVIVAL IN COURT

Crime Victim's Guide to Justice (2E)	$21.95
Grandparents' Rights (3E)	$24.95
Help Your Lawyer Win Your Case (2E)	$14.95
Jurors' Rights (2E)	$12.95
Legal Research Made Easy (2E)	$16.95
Winning Your Personal Injury Claim (2E)	$24.95
Your Rights When You Owe Too Much	$16.95

LEGAL SURVIVAL IN REAL ESTATE

Essential Guide to Real Estate Contracts	$18.95
Essential Guide to Real Estate Leases	$18.95
How to Buy a Condominium or Townhome (2E)	$19.95

LEGAL SURVIVAL IN PERSONAL AFFAIRS

Cómo Hacer su Propio Testamento	$16.95
Guía de Inmigración a Estados Unidos (3E)	$24.95
Guía de Justicia para Víctimas del Crimen	$21.95
Cómo Solicitar su Propio Divorcio	$24.95
How to File Your Own Bankruptcy (5E)	$21.95
How to File Your Own Divorce (4E)	$24.95
How to Make Your Own Will (2E)	$16.95
How to Write Your Own Living Will (2E)	$16.95
How to Write Your Own Premarital Agreement (3E)	$24.95
How to Win Your Unemployment Compensation Claim	$21.95
Living Trusts and Simple Ways to Avoid Probate (2E)	$22.95
Manual de Beneficios para el Seguro Social	$18.95
Most Valuable Personal Legal Forms You'll Ever Need	$24.95
Neighbor v. Neighbor (2E)	$16.95
The Nanny and Domestic Help Legal Kit	$22.95
The Power of Attorney Handbook (3E)	$19.95
Repair Your Own Credit and Deal with Debt	$18.95
The Social Security Benefits Handbook (3E)	$18.95
Unmarried Parents' Rights	$19.95
U.S.A. Immigration Guide (3E)	$19.95
Your Right to Child Custody, Visitation and Support (2E)	$24.95

Legal Survival Guides are directly available from Sourcebooks, Inc., or from your local bookstores.
Prices are subject to change without notice.

For credit card orders call 1–800–432–7444, write P.O. Box 4410, Naperville, IL 60567-4410
or fax 630-961-2168

SPHINX® PUBLISHING ORDER FORM

BILL TO:		SHIP TO:	
Phone #	Terms	F.O.B. Chicago, IL	Ship Date

Charge my: ☐ VISA   ☐ MasterCard   ☐ American Express

☐ **Money Order or Personal Check**

Credit Card Number

Expiration Date

Qty	ISBN	Title	Retail	Ext.
		SPHINX PUBLISHING NATIONAL TITLES		
	1-57248-148-X	Cómo Hacer su Propio Testamento	$16.95	
	1-57248-147-1	Cómo Solicitar su Propio Divorcio	$24.95	
	1-57248-166-8	The Complete Book of Corporate Forms	$24.95	
	1-57248-163-3	Crime Victim's Guide to Justice (2E)	$21.95	
	1-57248-159-5	Essential Guide to Real Estate Contracts	$18.95	
	1-57248-160-9	Essential Guide to Real Estate Leases	$18.95	
	1-57248-139-0	Grandparents' Rights (3E)	$24.95	
	1-57248-188-9	Guía de Inmigración a Estados Unidos (3E)	$24.95	
	1-57248-187-0	Guía de Justicia para Víctimas del Crimen	$21.95	
	1-57248-103-X	Help Your Lawyer Win Your Case (2E)	$14.95	
	1-57248-164-1	How to Buy a Condominium or Townhome (2E)	$19.95	
	1-57248-191-9	How to File Your Own Bankruptcy (5E)	$21.95	
	1-57248-132-3	How to File Your Own Divorce (4E)	$24.95	
	1-57248-100-5	How to Form a DE Corporation from Any State	$24.95	
	1-57248-083-1	How to Form a Limited Liability Company	$22.95	
	1-57248-099-8	How to Form a Nonprofit Corporation	$24.95	
	1-57248-133-1	How to Form Your Own Corporation (3E)	$24.95	
	1-57071-343-X	How to Form Your Own Partnership	$22.95	
	1-57248-119-6	How to Make Your Own Will (2E)	$16.95	
	1-57248-200-1	How to Register Your Own Copyright (4E)	$24.95	
	1-57248-104-8	How to Register Your Own Trademark (3E)	$21.95	
	1-57071-349-9	How to Win Your Unemployment Compensation Claim	$21.95	
	1-57248-118-8	How to Write Your Own Living Will (2E)	$16.95	
	1-57248-156-0	How to Write Your Own Premarital Agreement (3E)	$24.95	
	1-57248-158-7	Incorporate in Nevada from Any State	$24.95	
	1-57071-333-2	Jurors' Rights (2E)	$12.95	
	1-57071-400-2	Legal Research Made Easy (2E)	$16.95	
	1-57071-336-7	Living Trusts and Simple Ways to Avoid Probate (2E)	$22.95	

Qty	ISBN	Title	Retail	Ext.
	1-57248-186-2	Manual de Beneficios para el Seguro Social	$18.95	
	1-57248-167-6	Most Valuable Bus. Legal Forms You'll Ever Need (3E)	$21.95	
	1-57248-130-7	Most Valuable Personal Legal Forms You'll Ever Need	$24.95	
	1-57248-098-X	The Nanny and Domestic Help Legal Kit	$22.95	
	1-57248-089-0	Neighbor v. Neighbor (2E)	$16.95	
	1-57071-348-0	The Power of Attorney Handbook (3E)	$19.95	
	1-57248-149-8	Repair Your Own Credit and Deal with Debt	$18.95	
	1-57248-168-4	The Social Security Benefits Handbook (3E)	$18.95	
	1-57071-399-5	Unmarried Parents' Rights	$19.95	
	1-57071-354-5	U.S.A. Immigration Guide (3E)	$19.95	
	1-57248-138-2	Winning Your Personal Injury Claim (2E)	$24.95	
	1-57248-162-5	Your Right to Child Custody, Visitation and Support (2E)	$24.95	
	1-57248-157-9	Your Rights When You Owe Too Much	$16.95	
		CALIFORNIA TITLES		
	1-57248-150-1	CA Power of Attorney Handbook (2E)	$18.95	
	1-57248-151-X	How to File for Divorce in CA (3E)	$26.95	
	1-57071-356-1	How to Make a CA Will	$16.95	
	1-57248-145-5	How to Probate and Settle an Estate in California	$26.95	
	1-57248-146-3	How to Start a Business in CA	$18.95	
	1-57071-358-8	How to Win in Small Claims Court in CA	$16.95	
	1-57071-359-6	Landlords' Rights and Duties in CA	$21.95	
		FLORIDA TITLES		
	1-57071-363-4	Florida Power of Attorney Handbook (2E)	$16.95	
	1-57248-176-5	How to File for Divorce in FL (7E)	$26.95	
	1-57248-177-3	How to Form a Corporation in FL (5E)	$24.95	
	1-57248-086-6	How to Form a Limited Liability Co. in FL	$22.95	
	1-57071-401-0	How to Form a Partnership in FL	$22.95	
	1-57248-113-7	How to Make a FL Will (6E)	$16.95	

Form Continued on Following Page   **SUBTOTAL**

To order, call Sourcebooks at 1-800-432-7444 or FAX (630) 961-2168 (Bookstores, libraries, wholesalers—please call for discount)

Prices are subject to change without notice.

SPHINX® PUBLISHING ORDER FORM

Qty	ISBN	Title	Retail	Ext.
	1-57248-088-2	How to Modify Your FL Divorce Judgment (4E)	$24.95	
	1-57248-144-7	How to Probate and Settle an Estate in FL (4E)	$26.95	
	1-57248-081-5	How to Start a Business in FL (5E)	$16.95	
	1-57071-362-6	How to Win in Small Claims Court in FL (6E)	$16.95	
	1-57248-123-4	Landlords' Rights and Duties in FL (8E)	$21.95	

GEORGIA TITLES

Qty	ISBN	Title	Retail	Ext.
	1-57248-137-4	How to File for Divorce in GA (4E)	$21.95	
	1-57248-180-3	How to Make a GA Will (4E)	$21.95	
	1-57248-140-4	How to Start a Business in Georgia (2E)	$16.95	

ILLINOIS TITLES

Qty	ISBN	Title	Retail	Ext.
	1-57071-405-3	How to File for Divorce in IL (2E)	$21.95	
	1-57248-170-6	How to Make an IL Will (3E)	$16.95	
	1-57071-416-9	How to Start a Business in IL (2E)	$18.95	
	1-57248-078-5	Landlords' Rights & Duties in IL	$21.95	

MASSACHUSETTS TITLES

Qty	ISBN	Title	Retail	Ext.
	1-57248-128-5	How to File for Divorce in MA (3E)	$24.95	
	1-57248-115-3	How to Form a Corporation in MA	$24.95	
	1-57248-108-0	How to Make a MA Will (2E)	$16.95	
	1-57248-106-4	How to Start a Business in MA (2E)	$18.95	
	1-57248-107-2	Landlords' Rights and Duties in MA (2E)	$21.95	

MICHIGAN TITLES

Qty	ISBN	Title	Retail	Ext.
	1-57071-409-6	How to File for Divorce in MI (2E)	$21.95	
	1-57248-182-X	How to Make a MI Will (3E)	$16.95	
	1-57248-183-8	How to Start a Business in MI (3E)	$18.95	

MINNESOTA TITLES

Qty	ISBN	Title	Retail	Ext.
	1-57248-142-0	How to File for Divorce in MN	$21.95	
	1-57248-179-X	How to Form a Corporation in MN	$24.95	
	1-57248-178-1	How to Make a MN Will (2E)	$16.95	

NEW YORK TITLES

Qty	ISBN	Title	Retail	Ext.
	1-57248-141-2	How to File for Divorce in NY (2E)	$26.95	
	1-57248-105-6	How to Form a Corporation in NY	$24.95	
	1-57248-095-5	How to Make a NY Will (2E)	$16.95	
	1-57071-185-2	How to Start a Business in NY	$18.95	
	1-57071-187-9	How to Win in Small Claims Court in NY	$16.95	
	1-57071-186-0	Landlords' Rights and Duties in NY	$21.95	

Qty	ISBN	Title	Retail	Ext.
	1-57071-188-7	New York Power of Attorney Handbook	$19.95	
	1-57248-122-6	Tenants' Rights in NY	$21.95	

NORTH CAROLINA TITLES

Qty	ISBN	Title	Retail	Ext.
	1-57248-185-4	How to File for Divorce in NC (3E)	$22.95	
	1-57248-129-3	How to Make a NC Will (3E)	$16.95	
	1-57248-184-6	How to Start a Business in NC (3E)	$18.95	
	1-57248-091-2	Landlords' Rights & Duties in NC	$21.95	

OHIO TITLES

Qty	ISBN	Title	Retail	Ext.
	1-57248-190-0	How to File for Divorce in OH (2E)	$24.95	
	1-57248-174-9	How to Form a Corporation in OH	$24.95	
	1-57248-173-0	How to Make an OH Will	$16.95	

PENNSYLVANIA TITLES

Qty	ISBN	Title	Retail	Ext.
	1-57248-211-7	How to File for Divorce in PA (3E)	$26.95	
	1-57248-094-7	How to Make a PA Will (2E)	$16.95	
	1-57248-112-9	How to Start a Business in PA (2E)	$18.95	
	1-57071-179-8	Landlords' Rights and Duties in PA	$19.95	

TEXAS TITLES

Qty	ISBN	Title	Retail	Ext.
	1-57248-171-4	Child Custody, Visitation, and Support in TX	$22.95	
	1-57248-172-2	How to File for Divorce in TX (3E)	$24.95	
	1-57248-114-5	How to Form a Corporation in TX (2E)	$24.95	
	1-57071-417-7	How to Make a TX Will (2E)	$16.95	
	1-57071-418-5	How to Probate an Estate in TX (2E)	$22.95	
	1-57071-365-0	How to Start a Business in TX (2E)	$18.95	
	1-57248-111-0	How to Win in Small Claims Court in TX (2E)	$16.95	
	1-57248-110-2	Landlords' Rights and Duties in TX (2E)	$21.95	

SUBTOTAL THIS PAGE _____

SUBTOTAL PREVIOUS PAGE _____

Shipping — $5.00 for 1st book, $1.00 each additional _____

Illinois residents add 6.75% sales tax _____

Connecticut residents add 6.00% sales tax _____

TOTAL _____

To order, call Sourcebooks at 1-800-432-7444 or FAX (630) 961-2168 (Bookstores, libraries, wholesalers—please call for discount)

Prices are subject to change without notice.